AFTA SpringerBriefs in Family Therapy

A Publication of the American Family Therapy Academy

Founded in 1977, the **American Family Therapy Academy** is a non-profit organization of leading family therapy teachers, clinicians, program directors, policymakers, researchers, and social scientists dedicated to advancing systemic thinking and practices for families in their social context.

Vision

AFTA envisions a just world by transforming social contexts that promote health, safety, and well-being of all families and communities.

Mission

AFTA's mission is developing, researching, teaching, and disseminating progressive, just family therapy and family-centered practices and policies.

More information about this series at http://www.springer.com/series/11846

Robert Allan • Shruti Singh Poulsen
Editors

Creating Cultural Safety in Couple and Family Therapy

Supervision and Training

AFTA
American Family Therapy Academy

Springer

Editors
Robert Allan
School of Education and Human Development
University of Colorado Denver
Denver, CO, USA

Shruti Singh Poulsen
School of Education and Human Development
University of Colorado Denver
Denver, CO, USA

ISSN 2196-5528 ISSN 2196-5536 (electronic)
AFTA SpringerBriefs in Family Therapy
ISBN 978-3-319-64616-9 ISBN 978-3-319-64617-6 (eBook)
DOI 10.1007/978-3-319-64617-6

Library of Congress Control Number: 2017955547

Printed on acid-free paper

This Springer imprint is published by Springer Nature
The registered company is Springer International Publishing AG
The registered company address is: Gewerbestrasse 11, 6330 Cham, Switzerland

Series Foreword

The *AFTA Springer Briefs in Family Therapy* is an official publication of the American Family Therapy Academy. Each volume focuses on the practice and policy implications of innovative systemic research and theory in family therapy and allied fields. Our goal is to make information about families and systemic practices in societal contexts widely accessible in a reader friendly, conversational, and practical style. AFTA's core commitment to equality, social responsibility, and justice are represented in each volume.

Family therapy has a long history of innovative supervision and training that inspires the next generation of clinicians to see and work with systemic context of presenting issues and concerns. Our field is epistemologically well positioned to prepare clinicians to work sensitively and justly with persons across cultural contexts. How to do this work remains challenging and thinly charted. This volume, *Creating Cultural Safety in Couple and Family Therapy: Supervision and Training,* expands the notion of cultural competence from a static skill to a process of ongoing engagement. Editors Robert Allan and Shruti Singh Poulsen invite readers to consider cultural safety as a primary foundation for clinical work and supervision.

Chapter authors offer rich insight, detailed examples, and concrete suggestions for how to provide training and supervision responsive to the complex social ecologies among supervisor and supervisee, therapist and client. The authors are themselves culturally diverse and work in a range of settings. They generously share their own personal experiences, their research, and lessons learned as they grapple with how to do the work, day-to-day, context-to-context. Readers will find themselves reflecting on their own contexts, training models, and supervisory relationships and find useful practical ideas and guidelines that help transform aspirations regarding justice and cultural safety from theory to practice.

Lewis & Clark College
Portland, OR, USA

Carmen Knudson-Martin

Preface

Cultural Work in Clinical Supervision

We are pleased to be co-editing a volume that continues a rich dialogue about how to explore and integrate culture into our supervisory practices. We are faculty members in a Couple and Family Therapy specialization track within a Counseling program in Colorado, at a University in a major city. We are both AAMFT Approved Supervisors and couple and family therapists who engage in clinical work and supervision within and outside the academic setting. Robert is a second generation Canadian of northern European heritage, born and raised in Canada and he identifies as a cis-gendered, gay male. Shruti was born in India and is a first generation naturalized US citizen after immigrating to the US in her mid-teens. Shruti is an immigrant who has lived in several different countries other than the US and India, and identifies as a cis-gendered, heterosexual female.

For some clinicians, understanding culture as integral to clinical effectiveness is a seamless extension of their lives and practice. For others, there can be a mix of trying to link together training they have received with cultural considerations. Still others have a nascent awareness of some differences that emerge when working with new populations and a need to consider views that are different than their own. We are suggesting a move towards cultural safety as a means to explore how to incorporate this work in supervision.

Creating and maintaining cultural safety in supervision is an ongoing process that requires a supervisor to first establish an understanding of clinical work as cultural work, that they are a seamless part of each other, and then maintaining an ongoing engagement with how culture continuously weaves its way through a supervisee's clinical work and supervision itself. Much like sustaining a safe and supportive therapeutic or supervisory alliance; integrating culture in supervision is continuous and not a single moment in time or a single intervention. An unsafe cultural practice is an action that demeans the cultural identity of a particular person, couple or family. A cultural safety practice approach fits with a socially just approach to therapy and supervision by seeking to ensure equal social participation and promoting dignity, self-determination and well-being for all individuals, families, and communities.

Addressing cultural issues is considered an integral part of couple, family and systemic supervision work. There are a number of current training and supervision models that address multicultural competencies based on a defined list of what those competencies are (e.g. APA Guidelines on Multicultural Education, Training, Research, Practice and Organizational Change for Psychologists, AMCD Multicultural Counseling Competencies, AAMFT Approved Supervisor Requirements). However, descriptions of current models of culturally competent supervision are static in that they do not provide the lived experiences of supervisors who are attempting to do the very real work of culturally responsive and competent supervision with supervisees who are facing ever-changing and diverse client contexts. The static notion of competencies lacks contextual relevance for the lived realities of therapists and the complex social ecologies that clients live in. There has been a struggle to find a language that captures the fluidity of the constant and ever evolving work that recognizes culture at all levels of a system as central to clinical effectiveness. Various terms such as cultural attunement, cultural humility, culturally-infused, cultural equity and culturally-informed have all been utilized to counter the rigidity of a competency-based approach. Cultural competency training has been lauded as an effective, direct intervention to address the training of therapists and there is empirical support for the utilization of cultural competency training (Ibrahim & Heuer, 2016; Whaley & Davis, 2007). The major criticism of this training is the construct of competencies itself and the lack of understanding of the processes involved with engaging supervisees and learners in a life-long engagement with culture as integral to their work (Almeida, Dolan Del-Vecchio, & Parker, 2007). This volume makes an important contribution to cross-cultural competency in supervision because the authors present their supervision methods in a dynamic and culturally contextualized way, speaking both to their professional experiences as supervisors and to their personal journeys in developing and implementing clinical supervision methods.

Hardy (2016) provides a useful definition of culture as a "broad-based multidimensional concept that is comprised of, but not limited to, race, class, religion, sexual orientation, gender, family of origin, ethnicity, age, regionality" (p. 4). Hardy goes on to describe culture as simultaneously dynamic, fluid and static, a pervasive organizing principle, as multifaceted, and timeless. Part of our interest in this volume is the understanding that there are multiple perspectives on *culture*. We see this volume as having a heuristic value and generating further discussion about how to work with culture in supervision. This volume offers a range of perspectives, personal and professional, on addressing culture in supervision and training while providing concrete specifics of how to infuse supervision and training work with cultural realities.

The chapters in this volume offer a phenomenology of supervision that explores both the structures of experience and consciousness. The parts and the whole are explored and we encourage you to go back and forth between them, making your sense of what fits for your supervisory practice. The book offers a range of perspectives on addressing culture in supervision and training while offering concrete specifics of how to infuse supervision and training work with cultural realities of supervisors, supervisees, and clients. For supervisory practices to be effective, however, they have to be contextualized to the readers' own contexts. To that end, we encourage you to see the integration of culture into your supervision practices as continuous as opposed to a destination with a finite end and understand the limits of singular interventions intended to address a multitude of complexities in a population.

Clinical trainings, whether focused on self-of-therapist issues, or clinical skills development, or cultural competency, frequently are presented and received as a linear process with the result being participants "achieving" a concrete goal or outcome at their conclusion. One example of a training intervention intended to contribute to cultural safety is training which is designed for the purpose of creating a network of allies for LGBTQ students or employees in order to make a University or work community a safe and more supportive place. At the end of the workshop, participants get a rainbow sticker they can place on their door or in their office to indicate that they are an "ally" and that it is safe to discuss sexual orientation and gender related matters with them. This training is provided to all regardless of background or previous exposure to sexual orientation or gender related issues. The notion that a brief workshop provides all the knowledge, behavioral, and attitudinal attributes required to be culturally competent with at least four distinct and quite varied populations (L, G, B, and T) is an example of how limited a focus on a set of competencies can become. It also reflects how poorly some consider what the required competencies are for these populations. Therefore, our goal with this volume on culturally competent supervision is to emphasize the continuous, ongoing, and integrative nature of the clinical supervision process, one that is not discreet, finite, or limited to one chapter, one workshop, or a one-time learning experience in educational settings.

Integrating culture into our supervision work calls for a constant engagement and this book is intended to provide ways that one can engage and not with simplistic solutions but part of continuous entries into life-long conversations. As Manathunga (2011) notes, supervision "like any form of teaching and learning, is not a neutral intellectual zone" (p. 368). We bring our histories, gender, sexual orientation, class, race and cultural backgrounds into supervision. Much as Monk, Winslade, and Sinclair (2008) position counseling as cultural because it involves "the use of language, discourse, and concepts, each element of which is a product of a cultural world" (p. 449), we suggest that supervision is cultural as well.

This volume offers an array of ideas and specific approaches for working with a range of supervisees. Ladany, Mori, and Mehr (2013) reported that even the most effective supervisors combine effective and ineffective supervisor behaviors. Whether seasoned at working with culture in supervision or new to the role, the authors share experiences and perspectives that will prompt ideas for your supervision practice. Starting with a review of the relevant research literature, one of eh co-editors, Robert, presents what has been found to work for integrating culture into supervision. The research about this aspect of our field is limited and the author offers a broad agenda for research going forward.

The book continues with an engaging chapter from Laurel Salmon who is an LMFT and program supervisor at the Steinway Child and Family Services Marriage and Family Therapist Clinic. Salmon offers a reflexive framework that promotes a constant dialogue between people and environment not only for supervisees, but our own clinical and supervision practice. With the use of case examples and her own practice, Laurel models a humility about the process of supervision and trying to do our best work with clients. Next Shruti Singh Poulsen, the other co-editor, outlines a common factors approach to integrate systemic methods in supervision combined with MECA and the cultural genogram. Common factors have long been established as part of effective clinical work and Shruti shows how they can also be relevant for our supervision work.

Norma Scarborough passed away unexpectedly after submitting her chapter for this volume. We feel very fortunate to include her writing about the role of the racially underrepresented supervisor especially because so little writing is available from this perceptive. Norma offers her reflections on six areas from over twenty years of experience as a supervisor and explores challenges such as working with dominant culture supervisees and having her own expertise questioned. In the following chapter, Jessica ChenFeng and colleagues discuss a model for working with supervisees (CARE model (1) connecting with supervisees through sharing backgrounds/context; (2) appreciating privilege, power, and biases; (3) ratifying a cultural knowledge base with cultural humility; and (4) embracing our role as social justice agents). Their chapter offers specific questions and activities to use with supervisees.

Lana Kim and her co-authors describe the role of attunement to sociocultural emotion in supervision as a relational foundation for building and working with critical consciousness in supervision. They offer a range of ways to consider social locations of supervisees, clients, and the supervisor and how each engages in the change process in therapy. Ali Michael and Eleonora Bartoli then share a process for engaging graduate students in cultural training throughout their mental health training, thereby sidestepping the dilemma for the sole professor teaching "culture" which now becomes a shared responsibility across all faculty and courses. They describe a set of labs that form a foundation with graduate students for their education and their entire careers. We conclude this volume with a chapter by Toula Kourgiantakis and Marion Bogo from the University of Toronto. They clarify the distinction between cultural awareness and sensitivity and offer a critique of the cultural competency approach by explaining how a cultural competence approach overemphasizes cultural content and has insufficient emphasis on critical self-reflection and cultural sensitivity. They outline the use of the Objective Structured Clinical Examination (OSCE) as a means to frame the developmental process for students as well as supervisors.

The contributors to this volume have substantial experience as supervisors and educators and have generously shared their time and expertise here. We hope you enjoy this book as much as we did in bringing it together, and find it to be an important resource for supporting your clinical practice and supervision.

Denver, CO, USA

Robert Allan
Shruti Singh Poulsen

References

Almeida, R., Dolan Del-Vecchio, K., & Parker, L. (2007). *Transformative family therapy.* Boston, MA: Allyn & Bacon.

Hardy, K. V., & Bobes, T. (Eds.). (2016). *Culturally sensitive supervision and training: Diverse perspectives and practical applications.* New York, NY: Routledge.

Ibrahim, F. A., & Heuer, J. R. (2016). *Cultural and social justice counseling.* Basel, Switzerland: Springer.

Ladany N., Mori Y., Mehr K. E. (2013). Effective and ineffective supervision. *The Counseling Psychologist, 41*(1), 26–45. doi: 10.1177/0011000012442648

Manathunga, C. (2011). Moments of transculturation and assimilation: post-colonial explorations of supervision and culture. *Innovations in Education & Teaching International, 48*(4), 367–376. doi: 10.1080/14703297.2011.617089

Monk, G., Winslade, J., & Sinclair, S. (2008). *New horizons in multicultural counseling.* Los Angeles, CA: Sage.

Whaley, A. L., & Davis, K. E. (2007). Cultural competence and evidence-based practice in mental health services: A complementary perspective. *American Psychologist, 62*, 563–574. http://dx.doi.org/10.1037/0003-066X.62.6.563

Acknowledgments

We are grateful to the American Family Therapy Academy for highlighting the importance of the culture and multicultural competencies in clinical supervision of systemic therapies, and for sponsoring the AFTA Springer Briefs in Family Therapy. Thank you to Jennifer Hadley and the team at Springer Science for the guidance and support in the development of this volume. We also wish to give special thanks to Carmen Knudson-Martin for this opportunity to share our and other's work in cross-cultural clinical supervision; Carmen was instrumental in us taking on this project, providing with guidance and feedback throughout the process.

We are academics, clinicians, researchers, instructors, and clinical supervisors, as well as partners, family members, friends within our own cultural and social contexts. We are acutely aware of the multiple roles and responsibilities in which we engage in our personal and professional lives; these have an impact on us in our vision to be culturally responsive and competent supervisors and trainers. We are grateful to have this opportunity to share our work and challenges, as well as the work and creativity of other supervisors and trainers in this volume.

We extend heartfelt gratitude to each author who contributed to this book. Your creativity, commitment, and deep knowledge of yourselves personally and as clinicians and supervisors give us a combined work that is rich and diverse, and immediately applicable and relevant to our work as supervisors in systemic settings. Thank you for your responsiveness and follow through with the process of submission and revisions. We acknowledge the hard and thoughtful work of all supervisors who continually engage in self-reflection, improving their skills as supervisors, and take risks for the welfare of supervisees and clients because of their commitment to cross-cultural responsiveness and competence. This volume is really about and for them, and we are grateful for the opportunity to be able to give voice to this work of supervisors that is often invisible or "behind-the scenes."

Robert Allan
Shruti Singh Poulsen

Contents

Contributors

Eleonora Bartoli Graduate Counseling Program, Psychology Department, Arcadia University, Glenside, PA, USA

Marion Bogo Factor-Inwentash, Faculty of Social Work, University of Toronto, Toronto, ON, Canada

Marj Castronova Relational Wellness Institute, Las Vegas, NV, USA

Jessica ChenFeng Department of Educational Psychology & Counseling, California State University Northridge, Northridge, CA, USA

Lana Kim Department of Counseling Psychology, Lewis & Clark College, Portland, OR, USA

Toula Kourgiantakis Factor-Inwentash, Faculty of Social Work, University of Toronto, Toronto, ON, USA

Carmen Knudson-Martin Department of Counseling Psychology, Lewis and Clark College, Portland, OR, USA

Ali Michael Center for the Study of Race and Equity in Education, Graduate School of Education, University of Pennsylvania, Philadelphia, PA, USA

Laurel Salmon SCO Family of Services, Bronx, NY, USA

Norma Scarborough Alliant International University, Alhambra, CA, USA

Elisabeth Esmiol Wilson Department of Marriage and Family Therapy, Pacific Lutheran University, Tacoma, WA, USA

Toni Zimmerman Department of Human Development and Family Studies, Colorado State University, Fort Collins, CO, USA

About the Editors

Robert Allan, Ph.D., L.M.F.T., L.P.C. is an Assistant Professor in the couple and family track of the graduate counseling program at the University of Colorado Denver. He maintains an active clinical and supervisory practice and is an AAMFT and ICEEFT approved supervisor. His research interests include supervision, therapist learning and development, and attachment-based therapy approaches. He has published and presented on these topics and serves on the editorial board of two different research journals.

Shruti Singh Poulsen, Ph.D., L.M.F.T. is a scholar and clinician as well as an AAMFT Approved Supervisor whose work focuses on cross-cultural responsiveness in systemic clinical work and supervising and training culturally responsive and competent clinicians. She has published and presented extensively on topics related to the critical impact of culture and context on diverse client populations; these issues have included interracial relationships and families, immigration and its impact on couples and families, cultural contexts and evidence-based systemic practices, and impact of culture on clinical supervision. She serves on the editorial boards of the Journal of Marital and Family Therapy and the Journal of Couple and Relational Therapy. Her most recent cross-cultural experience of clinical work and supervision is in Istanbul, Turkey at Özyeğin University, as a Fulbright Senior Scholar, teaching and training in a newly-formed Couple and Family Therapy program.

Culture in Clinical Supervision: Research and Evidence

Robert Allan

Discussing culture is central to the supervision process for some supervisors and an opportunity to enter a discussion filled with landmines for others. Such different approaches to supervision can come to the fore as the relationship between a supervisor and supervisee evolves. The intention of this series is to present concise summaries of cutting-edge research and practical applications in family therapy and systemic practices. I teach, practice, and research couple and family therapy and supervision as an AAMFT Approved Supervisor and faculty member in a CACREP-accredited master's program in Colorado. As a second-generation Canadian of northern European heritage who was born and raised in Canada and identifies as a cis-gendered, gay male, integrating culture into my work is not a choice but a fact of my everyday life. This chapter draws on other supervision-related research I am conducting (Allan, McLuckie, & Hoffecker, 2016) and summarizes the themes in four areas: an overview of the research, what has been reported as effective for addressing culture in supervision, what the challenges are for addressing culture in supervision, and the research limitations. While there is substantive research available in languages other than English, I only have the capacity to review and present English-language research. Before reporting about the research, a note about the terminology has been used throughout this chapter.

Bernard and Goodyear (2014) note that supervision is an ongoing supportive learning process by which clinicians at all levels can develop, enhance, monitor and, when necessary, remediate professional functioning. Supervision's chief function is to minimize non-purposeful activity while maximizing intentionality. The goal is to optimize clinician competencies, ensure quality control, and enhance confidence to improve patient outcomes (Milne, 2009). Within the mental health field, clinical

R. Allan (✉)
School of Education and Human Development, University of Colorado Denver, Denver, CO, USA
e-mail: robert.allan@ucdenver.edu

R. Allan, S.S. Poulsen (eds.), *Creating Cultural Safety in Couple and Family Therapy*, AFTA SpringerBriefs in Family Therapy,
DOI 10.1007/978-3-319-64617-6_1

supervision is increasingly recognized as a core professional competency (Brosan, Reynolds, & Moore, 2008). It is now seen as an essential component both of modern effective health care systems (Kadushin, 2002) and of training programs for mental health therapists (Milne, Sheikh, Pattison, & Wilkinson, 2011; Watkins, 2011). Complicating things, however, is that each mental health profession has its own definition of supervision and of what the ethical and practice implications are for culturally competent practice. Similarly, each profession varies in terms of who is designated as a supervisor. For the purpose of this chapter, the term *supervisor* and *supervision* are intended to include all mental health professions and their definitions of supervision.

Supervision is a distinct professional practice with knowledge, skills, and attitudinal components. In some professions, specific training is required for a practitioner to be recognized as an "approved supervisor." The American Association of Marriage and Family Therapy, for example, has an "approved supervisor" designation that stipulates course work and 36 h of supervision among other requirements. Other professions promote experienced clinicians into the role of "supervisor" after gaining clinical experience over some period of time after receiving a license (Bernard & Goodyear, 2014; Falender, Burnes, & Ellis, 2013).

The research reviewed for this chapter included students and professors in graduate programs, licensure candidates and their supervisors, and mental health professionals involved in supervision activities post-licensure. Curiously, there is rarely a reference in the research literature to what supervision training supervisors received or the route by which they became designated as supervisors. This dearth may be due to the varied nature of the supervisor designation across professions.

Overview of the Research

Not surprisingly, much of what works for including culture in supervision is what has been found to also be good supervision practice overall. The working alliance, for example, between the supervisor and supervisee has to be strong with the supervisee feeling supported to explore a range of personal and clinical challenges that arise when working with clients. The supervisory relationship requires bi-directional trust and respect so that constructive feedback can both be delivered and received. Finally, good supervision requires time and an investment on behalf of the supervisor both to ensure client safety and meet the developmental needs of the supervisee (Campoli et al., 2016). As important as these aspects of successful supervision may be, the reality of the state of supervision in mental health fields is more complicated.

Falender and Shafranske (2004), in calling for increased instruction in this area, note that "many, if not most, supervisors practice without the benefit of education, training or supervision" (p. 7). A similar sentiment was repeated throughout the research literature, whether it was a call for supervisory competencies or enhanced or standardized training of supervisors. The realities for supervisors dealing with culture in supervision appear even more challenging with most training programs seeing issues of culture—if noted at all—as merely one area of competency (Bernard & Goodyear, 2014). The challenges are further complicated by what Manathunga (2011) refers to as an administrative discourse about supervision that focuses on roles and responsibilities, contracting, and goals; such approaches to supervision depict the practice of supervision as a form of project management. Issues of culture are not always wrapped up in one-line goal statements or neatly addressed on the forms noted as part of good supervisory practice from a project management perspective.

Milne et al. (2011) note the general lack of empirically tested theories and empirical knowledge about supervision overall. Instead, two prevalent ideologies emerge in the literature. One view calls for research to establish an evidence base for supervision in order to create an empirically based understanding of what is effective in supervision. Related to this approach is a call for a set of competencies that specifically define the practice of supervision (e.g., Falender & Shafranske, 2004). Having a common set of measurable competencies would be a precursor to establishing empirical knowledge about supervision. The second ideological approach to supervision suggests that supervisors and supervisees adopt a *lens* to view all clinical issues such as post-colonialism, feminist, multicultural, or post-modern. This outlook suggests a focus on supervisory processes that can encompass a wide range of clinical issues, contexts, and the developmental evolution of supervisees.

These two ideological positions are rooted in opposing epistemological and ontological understandings of a variety of issues, including what can and should be counted, what constitutes evidence, claims about truth, and whether people and systems can be broken down into measurable components. Given the experience with decades of dialogue about evidence-based practices in psychotherapy, we can expect discussions about evidence-based supervision to continue that are likely to be "controversial, resulting in frequent, passionate, and at times divisive debates in the field" (Sexton et al., 2011, p. 378). No one therapeutic approach is a panacea for all clinical issues; in a parallel process, mental health fields will benefit from ongoing, lively debate about what constitutes best supervisory practices.

When culture is addressed in supervision, both supervisors and supervisees describe the experience as more successful than if such issues are avoided, and the focus has a positive effect on the supervisory alliance (Butler, 2004; Burkard et al., 2006). Supervisees reported that the working relationship and satisfaction with supervisors were higher when supervisors took the lead in discussing the cultural differences between them (Gatmon et al., 2001). This in turn had a positive impact on supervisees' capacities to include culture in their own clinical work. Supervisees improved, for example, in their ability to integrate cultural issues in case treatment planning (Ladany, Inman, Constantine, & Hofheinz, 1997), in personal awareness of cultural issues (Toporek, Ortega-Villalobos, & Pope-Davis, 2004), and in overall case conceptualization abilities (Gainor & Constantine, 2002). They also reported developing higher levels of cultural competence when cultural issues were addressed as opposed to when they were not addressed in supervision (Falicov, 2014; Constantine, 2001).

Butler (2004) reports that supervisors who are well-versed in multicultural issues are more effective and it is incumbent on them to continually seek professional development in the knowledge and skills of multicultural supervision. Other researchers note that supervision is also influenced by a supervisor's previous experiences, including racial identity development. Ladany et al. (1997), for example, report that supervisory working alliances are stronger and the development of multicultural competence in supervisees is better when supervisor's racial identity development was equal to or higher than that of the supervisee. These researchers further reported that supervisees of color, in the face of internalized culturally unresponsive events from supervisors, reduce their disclosure and believe that a supervisor being culturally unresponsive has a negative impact on treatment.

Interestingly, supervisors are likely to report more discussion of cultural issues than do supervisees (Duan & Roehlke, 2001). Burkard et al. (2006) note the importance of supervisors taking the lead to set the tone for discussions about culture in supervision by asking questions about cultural issues and by considering how the client's cultural background may be influencing his or her presenting problem. Overall, when supervisees experience a growth-fostering relationship in supervision, they "increase their relational competencies" (Duffey, Haberstroh, Ciepcielinski, & Gonzales, 2016, p. 412), which supports their own development in working with a range of clients with compassion and mutuality.

What Is Effective for Addressing Culture in Supervision

A number of researchers have reported the importance of the supervisory alliance for exploring culture in supervision. Inman (2006), for example, noted that the perception by supervisees of a strong working alliance and of satisfaction with supervision by supervisees had a direct correlation to the probability of their exploring culture in supervision. Some researchers noted the importance of a contextualized working alliance, one that not only focused on relational safety both for the supervisee and for the supervisor, but which also requires co-construction of dialogical processes between supervisor and supervisee; the constant privileging of supervisee safety to allow for the exploration of challenging areas of clinical development reflects a limited view of power in supervision.

Hernández and McDowell (2010) explore the concept of relational safety in supervision as a foundation for integrating issues of culture and power on an ongoing basis in supervision. They see relational safety in supervision as co-constructed by all parties involved, with a focus on identities that "have been silenced by a lack of structural (material conditions) or discursive (social discourses) privilege" (p. 33). The emphasis is on the development of critical thinking in a supportive environment as opposed to blind validation or emotional support. Hernández and McDowell note that relational safety evolves over time as a result of each party taking responsibility for the risks assumed when supervisors and supervisees communicate with each other.

Adams (2009) reflects the need to address not only cultural issues in supervision but also issues related to power, thus promoting the idea that culture is not a powerless concept existing outside of any number of hierarchical implications for clients, supervisees, and supervisors. She proposed that specific time be set aside in supervision to discuss cultural differences and power hierarchies between supervisors and supervisees. Various other researchers have also reported that activities that promote both cultural and power understandings between supervisor and supervisee and the exploration by supervisees of their own cultural histories contribute to working effectively with culture in supervision.

Wong, Wong, and Ishiyama (2013) note the need for all those involved in supervision to explore worldviews, frames of reference, and tasks of supervision. Garcia, Kosutic, McDowell, and Anderson (2009) recommend specifically that supervisees do critical genograms to explore identities within a broader sociopolitical and historical context and that they should also complete questionnaires that explore social identities and systems of privilege and oppression (e.g., the Privilege and Oppression Inventory). The cultural genogram (Hardy & Laszloffy, 1995) is another training tool used to promote both cultural awareness and sensitivity, while Hernández and McDowell (2010) suggest the use of films, books, song lyrics, and documentaries as part of an ongoing exploration that promotes greater dialogue about culture in supervision.

Ancis and Marshall (2010) review a wide range of areas of supervision from supervisor/ee-focused development through to evaluation of the supervisory process. Starting with supervisor/ee-focused personal development, the authors note that supervisors: proactively introduce cultural issues in supervision; actively disclose own cultural background, biases, and experiences; are aware of clinical impact of racism and oppression; facilitate supervisee's exploration of the influence of their cultural background on clients and explore own cultural lenses; and, encourage supervises to increase own cultural awareness. For the conceptualization domain, Ancis and Marshall (2010) reported that supervisors both encourage trainees to consider the client's perspective about his or her problem before making clinical judgments and encourage supervisees to consider client's role in goal setting. For interventions, supervisors encourage supervisee to facilitate client's awareness of social issues and conveyed an acceptance of cultural differences. In terms of the process of supervision, Ancis and Marshall note that supervisors facilitate a safe relationship with supervisees and initiate and engage in discussions of power dynamics. Finally, for evaluation, supervisors identify supervisees' multicultural strengths and emphasize that cultural discussions positively affect clinical outcomes.

For her part, Estrada (2006) described the supervisor as cultural broker supporting supervisees to explore value conflicts that stem from cultural beliefs to develop coherence in order for the supervisee to engage in constructive and supportive dialogue with clients. Hernández and Rankin (2008) review such a process, using sexual orientation as an example. In a group supervision context, they recommend starting with delineating those who need to become aware of privilege and those who need to develop confidence in speaking about their lived experiences as a sexual minority. Confronting privilege can include challenging dialogical exchanges about multiple identities, as a supervisor encourages an understanding of both one's own privilege and of being accountable for one's own power position and privilege. Next, group participants explore how privilege can play out in multiple ways including how theories and clinical practice are accountable for homophobia. Finally, supervisors promoting self-definition for clients can expand clinical discussions beyond labels (diagnostic and identifying) that limit the understanding of the clients' relational world.

Challenges When Addressing Culture in Supervision

Overall, there is limited research about any kind of supervision, let alone dealing specifically with culture in supervision. The limited research remains one of the largest challenges for better understanding how best to comprehensively integrate culture into the supervisory process (Falender et al., 2013). The bulk of the existing research is either survey-based or case studies. It is also apparent that there is tremendous variation in how professions and training programs attend to culture as an integral part of the profession. The reality that culture was either one course or a chapter in a text book in graduate training programs or supervision training was repeated by several researchers (Falender, Shafranske, & Falicov, 2014).

Other challenges noted in the research are supervisee readiness and resistance. Butler (2004) noted that supervisors must be prepared to focus on, and work through, resistance when supervisees are struggling with aspects of cultural competence. Resistance from supervisees, supervisees feeling overwhelmed, or—to put it in less laden terms—supervisees' learning and developing will always be a part of understanding how culture is both part of and influences our clinical work. The challenges or "resistance" cannot be avoided and they provide excellent opportunities for supervisors to model appropriate behavior and responses, while at the same time promoting an open and genuine dialogue with supervisees (Butler, 2004).

While the exploration of cultural issues is critical for the development of competency (Helms & Cook, 1999), supervisee readiness and styles of communication are also a challenge in addressing culture in supervision. Killian (2001) reported that directive vs. collaborative styles of communication have an impact on the tasks and goals of supervision. Supervisees may not view developing cultural competence a priority in supervision. Similarly, they may not consider greater self-disclosure from the supervisor to be a gateway to their own exploration of internalized stereotypes. Various forms of identity development will influence the degree to which both supervisors and supervisees can explore culture in supervision. Killian, for example, further noted that supervisors with higher racial consciousness than their supervisees seem better equipped to attend to these issues in supervision and to develop a culturally receptive environment.

The Research Limitations

As previously noted, there is limited research in the mental health fields about how best to integrate culture into supervision, and much of the research that has been done is survey-based (Burkard et al., 2006). Research is particularly lacking about the diversity and cultural aspects of supervising trainees with disabilities (Andrews et al., 2013). Similarly, there is paucity of research about international and cross-national supervision (Son, Ellis, & Yoo, 2013). Further research is also required about the need to attend to multiple identities in supervision and on the development of different research approaches that are culturally intentional and social justice-oriented (Hernández & McDowell, 2010).

Surprisingly, in the existing research, among any number of factors that we have come to expect when reviewing research about various clinical approaches, information is very often missing on some of the seemingly most obvious issues. What training have supervisors received? How did supervisors gain the designation of "supervisor?" What type of supervision were they providing? How long were the supervision sessions? How many hours of supervision were provided? Was the supervision recorded and assessed for its quality? The lack of such information may be why some are calling for either a competency-based approach to supervision or evidence-based supervision.

Milne and Reiser (2012) provide a rationale for evidence-based supervision that includes quality control and "fitness for practice." These authors review various arguments that are generally made for any evidence-based approaches to clinical work. They contend, for example, that taking an evidence-based approach to supervision would promote a methodological stance for supervision practice, encourage a disciplined approach to the training of supervisors, and would create accountability mechanisms for funders, policy makers, and programs.

Falender et al. (2013) focus their writing on the need for a competency-based approach to multicultural supervision and on the need to develop competencies that can be measured and researched. Starting with a definition of competency which incorporates related professional ethics and a competency cube (Rodolfa et al., 2005) that identifies foundational and functional competencies, Falendar and co-authors outline a series of competencies for effective multicultural supervision. These supervision competencies build on competency statements about effective multicultural clinical practice and attend to knowledge, skill, self-identity awareness, and process domains.

When an aspect of a field is in its nascent stages, it is important to support the development of initial ideas and one is hesitant to critique what is being proposed for fear of limiting the development of new ideas. The critiques of evidence-based approaches and lists of competencies are, however, well-established (e.g., Midgley, 2009), and the same applies to seeing the practice of supervision as a singular, replicable practice that can be measured. The notion that being competency-based can then lead to the development of related empirical research limits our scope of knowledge and replicates colonizing approaches to epistemology. This author advocates for a both/and approach. Such an approach can respond to the imperatives of best practices, codes of ethics, and licensing processes which lead us to reify lists of competencies, while at the same time seeking out supervision practices that do more than merely create a waterline that we continually bob around to assess whether the adequate level of supervision has been reached without any forces compelling us to supervisory innovation and responsiveness that is needed to be truly culturally responsive.

Conclusion

Ancis and Marshall (2010) report that when cultural variables are attended to in the supervisory relationship, the supervision experience is more enjoyable and the supervisor is seen as more credible. Other researchers have noted that as a result of interactions with culturally competent supervisors, the cultural awareness of supervisees is increased, which, in turn, affects how they incorporate supervisory suggestions and multiculturalism into their own client sessions (Toporek et al., 2004). While the research about how best to integrate culture into supervision is in the early stages of development at this point in time, there is extensive case- and survey-based research to draw on to develop an understanding of how best to continually integrate culture in supervision.

Learning to further integrate culture into supervision is a trial and error process, and like learning, a new therapy approach requires attention to specific tasks while learning to integrate these specific tasks into an overall coherent approach (Allan, Ungar, & Eatough, 2016). This volume offers a number of specific ideas about what to do as well as raises a number of questions to consider as a supervisor. As you read this volume, pay attention to your own reactions to the different strategies proposed and ask yourself questions about how they fit for your supervisory approach as well as read them as an interrogation of your supervisory approach. This is an opportunity to have a reflexive dialogue with the authors' writing as a means to engage in the ongoing development seen as the hallmark of good clinical practice.

References

Adams, D. M. (2009). Multicultural pedagogy in the supervision and education of psychotherapists. *Women & Therapy, 33*(1-2), 42–54. doi:10.1080/02703140903404713

Allan, R., McLuckie, A., & Hoffecker, L. (2016). Title for a systematic review: Clinical supervision of psychotherapists: A systematic review. In *Campbell collaboration*. Retrieved from http://www.campbellcollaboration.org/lib/project/365/

Allan, R., Ungar, M., & Eatough, V. (2016). "So I feel like I'm getting it and then sometimes I think OK, no I'm not": Couple and family therapists learning an evidence-based practice. *Australian and New Zealand Journal of Family Therapy, 37*, 56–74. doi:10.1002/anzf.1134

Ancis, J. R., & Marshall, D. S. (2010). Using a multicultural framework to assess supervisees' perceptions of culturally competent supervision. *Journal of Counseling & Development, 88*(3), 277–284. doi:10.1002/j.1556-6678.2010.tb00023.x

Andrews, E. E., Kuemmel, A., Williams, J. L., Pilarski, C., Dunn, M., & Lund, E. M. (2013). Providing culturally competent supervision to trainees with disabilities in rehabilitation settings. *Rehabilitation Psychology,58*(3), 233–244. doi:10.1037/a0033338.

Bernard, J. M., & Goodyear, R. K. (2014). *Fundamentals of clinical supervision* (5th ed.). Boston, MA: Pearson.

Brosan, L., Reynolds, S., & Moore, R. G. (2008). Self-evaluation of cognitive therapy performance: Do therapists know how competent they are? *Behavioural Cognitive Psychotherapy, 36*(5), 581–587. doi:10.1017/S1352465808004438

Burkard, A. W., Johnson, A. J., Madson, M. B., Pruitt, N. T., Contreras-Tadych, D. A., Kozlowski, J. M., et al. (2006). Supervisor cultural responsiveness and unresponsiveness in cross-cultural supervision. *Journal of Counseling Psychology, 53*(3), 288–301. doi:10.1037/0022-0167.53.3.288

Butler, S. K. (2004). Multicultural sensitivity and competence in the clinical supervision of school counselors and school psychologists. *The Clinical Supervisor, 22*(1), 125–141. doi:10.1300/J001v22n01_09

Campoli, J., Cummings, J., Heidt, C., O'Connell, M. E., Mossière, A., & Pierce, A. (2016). Top 5 components of "good enough" supervision. *The Society for the Advancement of Psychotherapy*. Retrieved from http://societyforpsychotherapy.org/top-5-components-good-enough-supervision

Constantine, M. G. (2001). Multiculturally-focused counseling supervision: Its relationship to trainees' multicultural counseling self-efficacy. *The Clinical Supervisor, 20*(1), 87–98. doi:10.1300/J001v20n01_07

Duan, C., & Roehlke, H. (2001). A descriptive "snapshot" of cross-racial supervision in university counseling center internships. *Journal of Multicultural Counseling and Development, 29*(2), 131–146. doi:10.1002/j.2161-1912.2001.tb00510.x

Duffey, T., Haberstroh, S., Ciepcielinski, E., & Gonzales, C. (2016). Relational-cultural theory and supervision: Evaluating developmental relational counseling. *Journal of Counseling & Development, 94*(4), 405–414. doi:10.1002/jcad.12099

Estrada, D. (2006). Supervision sensitivity: Impact of supervisors' ethnic origin on exploration of counselors' cultural competency. *The Guidance and Counselling Journal, 21*(1), 14–20.

Falender, C. A., Burnes, T. R., & Ellis, M. V. (2013). Multicultural clinical supervision and benchmarks: Empirical support informing practice and supervisor training. *The Counseling Psychologist, 41*(1), 8-27. doi.org/10.1177/0011000012438417.

Falender, C. A., Shafranske, E. P., & Falicov, C. (2014). Diversity and multiculturalism in supervision. In C. A. Falender, E. P. Shafranske, & C. Falicov (Eds.), *Multiculturalism and diversity in clinical supervision: A competency-based approach* (pp. 3–28). Washington, DC: American Psychological Association.

Falender, C. A., & Shafranske, E. P. (2004). *Clinical supervision: A competency-based approach.* Washington, DC: American Psychological Association.

Falicov, C. J. (2014). Psychotherapy and supervision as cultural encounters: The MECA framework. In C. A. Falender, E. P. Shafranske, & C. J. Falicov (Eds.), *Multiculturalism and diversity in clinical supervision: A competency-based approach* (pp. 29–58). Washington, DC: American Psychological Association.

Gainor, K. A., & Constantine, M. G. (2002). Multicultural group supervision: A comparison of in-person versus web-based formats. *Professional School Counseling, 6*(2), 104–111. http://www.jstor.org/stable/42732399

Garcia, M., Kosutic, I., McDowell, T., & Anderson, S. (2009). Raising critical consciousness in family therapy supervision. *Journal of Feminist Family Therapy, 21*, 18–38.

Gatmon, D., Jackson, D., Koshkarian, L., Martos-Perry, N., Molina, A., Patel, N., et al. (2001). Exploring ethnic, gender, and sexual orientation variables in supervision: Do they really matter? *Journal of Multicultural Counseling and Development, 29*(2), 102–113. doi:10.1002/j.2161-1912.2001.tb00508.x

Hardy, K. V., & Laszloffy, T. A. (1995). The cultural genogram: Key to training culturally competent family therapists. *Journal of Marital and Family Therapy, 21*(3), 227–237. doi:10.1111/j.1752-0606.1995.tb00158.x

Helms, J. E., & Cook, D. A. (1999). *Using race and culture in counseling and psychotherapy: Theory and process*. Boston, MA: Allyn & Bacon.

Hernández, P., & McDowell, T. (2010). Intersectionality, power, and relational safety in context: Key concepts in clinical supervision. *Training and Education in Professional Psychology, 4*(1), 29–35. doi:10.1037/a0017064

Hernández, P., & Rankin, P. (2008). Relational safety and liberating training spaces: An application with a focus on sexual orientation issues. *Journal of Marital and Family Therapy, 34*(2), 251–264. doi:10.1111/j.1752-0606.2008.00067.x

Inman, A. G. (2006). Supervisor multicultural competence and its relation to supervisory process and outcome. *Journal of Marital and Family Therapy, 32*(1), 73–85. doi:10.1111/j.1752-0606.2006.tb01589.x

Kadushin, A. (2002). *Supervision in social work* (4th ed.). New York, NY: University Press.

Killian, K. D. (2001). Differences making a difference: Cross-cultural interactions in supervisory relationships. *Journal of Feminist Family Therapy, 12*(2-3), 61–103. doi:10.1300/J086v12n02_03

Ladany, N., Inman, A. G., Constantine, M. G., & Hofheinz, E. W. (1997). Supervisee multicultural case conceptualization ability and self-reported multicultural competence as functions of supervisee racial identity and supervisor focus. *Journal of Counseling Psychology, 44*(3), 284–293. doi:10.1037/0022-0167.44.3.284

Manathunga, C. (2011). Moments of transculturation and assimilation: Post-colonial explorations of supervision and culture. *Innovations in Education & Teaching International, 48*(4), 367–376. doi:10.1080/14703297.2011.617089

Midgley, N. (2009). Editorial: Improvers, adapters and rejecters the link between 'evidence-based practice' and 'evidence-based practitioners'. *Clinical Child Psychology and Psychiatry, 14*(3), 323–327. doi:10.1177/1359104509104045

Milne, D. (2009). *Evidence-based clinical supervision: Principles and practices*. London, UK: Wiley-Blackwell.

Milne, D., & Reiser, R. P. (2012). A rationale for evidence-based clinical supervision. *Journal of Contemporary Psychotherapy, 42*, 139–149. doi:10.1007/s10879-011-9199-8

Milne, D. L., Sheikh, A. I., Pattison, S., & Wilkinson, A. (2011). Evidence-based training for clinical supervisors: A systematic review of 11 controlled studies. *The Clinical Supervisor, 30*(1), 53–71. doi:10.1080/07325223.2011.564955

Rodolfa, E., Bent, R., Eisman, E., Nelson, P., Rehm, L., & Ritchie, P. (2005). A cube model for competency development: Implications for psychology educators and regulators. *Professional Psychology: Research and Practice, 36*, 347–354. doi:10.1037/0735-7028.36.4.347

Sexton, T., Gordon, K. C., Gurman, A., Lebow, J., Holtzworth-Munroe, A., & Johnson, S. (2011). Guidelines for classifying evidence-based treatments in couple and family therapy. *Family Process, 50*(3), 377–392. doi:10.1111/j.1545-5300.2011.01363.x

Son, E. J., Ellis, M. V., & Yoo, S. K. (2013). Clinical supervision in South Korea and the United States: A comparative descriptive study. *The Counseling Psychologist, 41*(1), 48–65. doi:10.1177/0011000012442650

Toporek, R. L., Ortega-Villalobos, L., & Pope-Davis, D. B. (2004). Critical incidents in multicultural supervision: Exploring supervisees' and supervisors' experiences. *Journal of Multicultural Counseling and Development, 32*(2), 66–83. doi:10.1002/j.2161-1912.2004.tb00362.x

Watkins, C. E., Jr. (2011). Does psychotherapy supervision contribute to patient outcomes? Considering thirty years of research. *The Clinical Supervisor, 30*(2), 235–256. doi:10.1080/07325223.2011.619417

Wong, L. J., Wong, P. P., & Ishiyama, F. (2013). What helps and what hinders in cross-cultural clinical supervision: A critical incident study. *The Counseling Psychologist, 41*(1), 66–85. doi:10.1177/0011000012442652

The Four Questions: A Framework for Integrating an Understanding of Oppression Dynamics in Clinical Work and Supervision

Laurel Salmon

I have always been interested in oppression and how it creates power dynamics in relationships, both professional and personal. Like most people, my unique identity gives me differing levels of privilege. As a woman of color, I experience being marginalized on a daily basis. However, as a person who is identified as straight and cisgendered, I also experience privilege. I am often not even aware that I am experiencing that privilege. Systems of oppression function without me doing anything to benefit from my privilege besides just living my everyday life (Van Kerk, Smith, & Andrew, 2011). Initially, as a clinician and then as a supervisor, I have always been concerned with how power dynamics and attitudes shaped by oppression impact our work.

When I look at my relationships and interactions, the ones that are the most meaningful are the ones where I do not have to censor myself. These are the relationships where I can be forthcoming about all of my experiences. The relationships where I cannot do that are the ones that sometimes feel are leaving out a significant portion of who I am as a person. My ability to discuss oppression may or may not be impactful in friendships. Every relationship does not have to go that deep. In therapeutic relationships, however, the ability to honestly look at how clients experience the world due to their unique social identities is very impactful. These relationships are, by definition, deep. What does it mean for our work if we are overlooking or ignoring a large factor in how our clients are functioning? If the system exists without us actively doing anything other than living our lives, how are we acting it out with our clients?

L. Salmon (✉)
SCO Family of Services, Bronx, NY, USA
e-mail: laurelmsalmon@gmail.com

R. Allan, S.S. Poulsen (eds.), *Creating Cultural Safety in Couple and Family Therapy*, AFTA SpringerBriefs in Family Therapy,
DOI 10.1007/978-3-319-64617-6_2

Juanita*

Juanita was an 11-year-old Latina female and she lived with her older sister, who was her legal guardian. Before being assigned to me, she had seen three other therapists in our clinic. Her sister had a reputation for being less than forthcoming and at times difficult to work with. When I met them for their first session, she was somewhat abrupt, but it was evident to me that she cared deeply about her sister. When I met Juanita alone, she was cooperative and friendly. Juanita's sister was diagnosed with breast cancer shortly after she became my client. She hired a babysitter to bring her to sessions, and I rarely saw her. When I attempted to contact the sister for more information, she artfully avoided any discussion of their parents. There was a lot of focus on Juanita's behavioral issues and on how her sister's illness impacted her. She was acting out in school and needed to improve her social skills. She was having tremendous difficulties relating to her peers and had a very high level of distress about it. Her sister was her legal guardian and Juanita mentioned once in a session that she had never met her mother. The most she said was that she called from Ecuador, and her sister would get sad during the phone calls. She was always very guarded when the topic shifted to her family, and it was not part of her treatment planning.

When we talked in therapy about her difficulty following rules in school and what the consequences could be for that, she would make jokes. She often joked about going to jail and talked about how she did not want to go there. From therapy sessions, I often remember the things my clients say, but I do not always remember my responses. I know that her jokes about jail were an ongoing theme for a while, but it was never the biggest part of the session, so it never actually got investigated. One day about a year into our time together, Juanita came into my office and was very quiet. It was a struggle to get her to engage, and she did not have her usual sense of playfulness. She was like this for most of the session, and when I questioned her about it, she just shrugged. I continued attempting to distract her. When she won a card game we were playing, I very dramatically insisted that we both do a victory dance to celebrate. She started to come around. I reminded her that if something was bothering her, she could tell me. She replied that she was not supposed to tell anyone her "business." So I explained to her that therapy is a place where you can tell people your "business" and no one ever has to know. We had, of course, talked about this before, but she finally had a real context for it. I explained to her that unless she was in danger of being hurt or hurting herself, whatever she told me was a secret. Visibly relieved, she admitted to me that she went to visit her father in prison that previous weekend. She revealed that she had been going to visit him in prison as far back as she could remember. She said she had never told anyone before because she was embarrassed and her sister told her that it was their biggest secret. I asked her why she felt like she could tell me. She said that she knew I did not think someone was a bad person just because they were in jail. She is right, I do believe this, but I have no idea how I conveyed this to her. Somehow I did because she never felt like she could tell another person this. It made me realize how long she had been carrying around this secret and how if I had not somehow sent her the message that I would be a person she could talk with about wither father being in prison, that there was a huge part of her that I might not have ever seen in therapy. She came in the next week and told me that she talked to her sister and said that her sister told her that it would be alright for her to keep talking to me about her father. Juanita's father was incarcerated for selling drugs 7 years ago. She had so many bad experiences talking about it that she just stopped talking about it with anyone who was not already aware of her father's incarceration. She said that people judge him. They assume he is "a lowlife" or "a deadbeat" and they judge the entire family. Juanita's sister very poignantly said to me that when there is a story on the news about someone selling drugs or committing any crime, there is rarely any backstory about how hard it is for Black men to get jobs to support their families. "No one ever assumes that he was desperate after being unemployed for an extended period. Instead, people think that I don't know how to raise Juanita or that I should keep her away from our father. They constantly ask me if he was in a gang or if he was abusive. People also ask me if he molested us! No one wants to believe he is a good person who loves us. So we just don't talk about it."

Over time, I was able to work with them in family sessions about their feelings regarding their father and how they reconciled their ideas about him with what the world assumed about him. It was some of the best work I have ever done, and I cannot believe that I could have easily done something in a session that would have caused me to miss out on doing that work. What became apparent to me is that the same way I conveyed something that made them feel safe, others before me had expressed the opposite—most likely without even realizing it because we all want to help our clients; this is why we do this work. I wanted to make sure that I was always approaching clients the same way that I was approaching Juanita.

"The Four Questions" is a framework that reminds the clinician how messages in our culture impact how we view people and brings us back to the oppression analysis context. I wanted a structure that could give a starting point for looking at clients. I also wanted to be able to refer to when we needed to refocus our lens. To test the framework, I chose one of the most challenging cases I had. I took a case that involved multiple oppressions that often intersected.

Velma

Velma is a 49–year-old married, African American mother of two. She has been in recovery for 8 years from a long battle with addiction to crack cocaine. Velma was married to a man who abused and prostituted her for many years to support his drug habit. She started smoking crack to survive the abuse as well as the many horrors she experienced being forced into sex work. Five years after getting off of crack (without a program), she immediately realized that being out on the streets at night was not an option. Velma started to suffer from crippling anxiety and PTSD and her life as a prostitute ended. She helped her husband get clean and hoped that the abuse she endured would stop, but it seemingly got worse. When she became my client, there was an open investigation with the city's Child Welfare Services (CWS) because her children had missed an excessive amount of school and her older daughter had been caught in the school bathroom cutting her arms. When I spoke with the CWS caseworker assigned to the family, she said that there had been a history of not being compliant with agency demands. She also stated that the children had been removed from the home previously when my client was actively abusing drugs and that made it more likely to happen again. When I asked the caseworker to elaborate on what she meant by "lack of cooperation," she admitted that the mother had complied with everything. She had taken two parenting classes and completed a drug counseling program (which they required even though she never failed one of the 14 drug tests they had administered). They mandated counseling for both parents; my client had been going fairly regularly except for when she had severe episodes of anxiety that prevented her from leaving the house. However, the father was openly belligerent in court and refused to comply with any demands set by the judge. The father regularly missed appointments made for him for drug testing and openly stated that he would not go to any programs assigned to him. He was frequently witnessed yelling at his lawyer, the CWS worker, and case worker assigned to him. I asked CWS what options my client had if she cannot get him to comply. I was fairly confident that if the judge and CWS could not make him comply that my client had even less of a chance.

The CWS worker was silent for several seconds and then finally said, "Well if she wants to keep her kids, she needs to get him to cooperate." So I asked again, "what if she cannot get him to cooperate?" She paused and then asked if I thought they needed couples therapy to work out their "relationship difficulties." I would not suggest couples work for cases of domestic violence, but confidentiality barred me from stating that.

The notes from the previous therapist stated that he had tried to do some work with Velma about domestic violence, but she was adamant that it should not be revealed to CWS, and she had refused to call the police. The previous therapist had been puzzled by that and suspected that maybe she was exaggerating it. Therefore, he stopped even talking about domestic violence with the assumption that if things were "dangerous," she would be more "proactive" about it. Based on how her husband was behaving with people outside the relationship, I did not have any illusions about how bad it was for her. I just needed to figure out how I could use that knowledge to help her.

The Four Questions Framework

1. What are the common stereotypes about each of the groups that she falls into?
2. What is the dynamic between us because of oppression?
3. How can I expect to oppress her inadvertently if I am not careful?
4. How are the current presenting problems related to oppression?

The first thing that I need to do with this client is "locate" her in oppression structures:

- African American
- Woman
- Domestic violence victim
- Mental illness
- Substance abuse
- Public assistance recipient
- Prostitution

As with the previous case, each of these descriptors, whether current or in the past, comes with many assumptions that can shape how I think about her. Whether I want to believe that they influence me or not, this is true. All of the systems she is involved with treat her according to those assumptions as well. That is just how she experiences the world.

What Are the Common Stereotypes About Each of the Groups That She Falls Into?

What might I think about her situation because of these assumptions? What do I have to do in therapy to make sure that I do not project any of these assumptions on her? With this, the first step is acknowledging that these assumptions go along with these labels. The second phase is actively thinking about not defining her that way.

In my first session with Velma, I asked her to tell me a little bit about what brought her to the office. She began to tell me about her childhood and mental health history. I noticed that we were not talking about the current situation with CWS or the danger of having her children removed. She had been dealing with the investigation for 4 months when she came to see me. I imagined that she had a lot of thoughts and feelings about what was happening to her, which she probably was not given space to express. I asked her what it was like to have her parenting judged by others. I meant CWS and family court, but I left it open-ended. She avoided the question by telling me about the parenting class that she was taking. She started going through one of the bags that she brought into the room and pulled out a black and white notebook. She began to read to me all kinds of plans that she had written up for the kids. She had created daily schedules of activities including art classes, dance classes, and karate. There was a list of learning enrichment books that she was going to buy to help them study. She even had plans for how she would redecorate their rooms. There were several directions where I could have gone with what she was putting in the room at that moment. It was tempting to ask her if she thought all of her plans were realistic given her financial situation. She stated earlier in the session that she had no income. She was on food stamps and Medicaid. Then there was also the issue of her ability to get her children to all of these places when she sometimes experienced crippling anxiety and could not leave the house. It also went through my mind if I should ask her if a book full of activities was what her children needed at the moment. I also wondered if she was just telling me what she thought I wanted to hear and exaggerating or lying.

Then I realized that I might be making an assumption about her because of some of the labels that had been attached to her. Instead, I decided not to comment at all, and before the next session, I asked myself a few questions. Do I think she is a bad parent? If she was not involved in an open CWS case with the history of substance abuse, prostitution, and domestic violence, would I have any judgment about her planning activities for her children? When we think about people who are in danger having their children taken away, we usually believe that they must have done something wrong. What if instead, I assumed that she was a good, well-meaning parent until she proved otherwise?

Do I think she is not trustworthy? Do I think she is not reliable or credible? What if she fully intended to take her children to all of these activities and had figured out ways to do this in her community? Before I make assumptions about her not telling the truth or the impossibility of her affording these activities, I needed just to be curious. When I asked my students or my clinicians in discussion groups about common traits of substance abusers, "they lie" is always one of the first three items listed. Was I assuming that she could not possibly be telling the truth? What about as a woman of color? Did I assume that she was less than truthful because of that? She has a history of prostitution, and there was clearly domestic violence in her relationship at one point, even if it was not confirmed to be going on now. Did I think she made poor choices?

I opted not to bring any of these things up. Instead, I thought about why it was so important to her to show me her notebook, especially in the first meeting. What might she be trying to tell me and why? In the next session, I chose to ask her if she was afraid that I thought she was a bad mother. She immediately started to cry. So I invited her to consider allowing me to prove to her that I was not going to judge her. I believe that took our work in a new direction than where she had gone before.

What Are the Dynamics Between Us because of Oppression?

How is this client routinely oppressed by helping systems? What does this client probably think about me? Does the client worry that I am on the side of CWS who she experiences as calling her a bad parent or a criminal? Does she think that there are huge class issues? Does she expect me to understand her lifestyle? Does she expect me to understand domestic violence? Is she afraid to tell me things because she thinks I will tell CWS? What kind of treatment does she expect from me? (Does she expect me to talk down to her? Does she expect me to see or hear her as a person?)

Looking back now, it seems obvious that she might worry about me judging her. As therapists, we are put in the role of judging our clients and the role they play in their problems. If we did not think that we could improve client's lives through transforming them, then there would be little point to being in the room with them. However, there is a fine line between creating space for change and blaming them for the situations that they are in. We can often cross that line without meaning it or even realizing it. The power that we have as the perceived expert can make us influence client's lives in ways that can be scary to them and even to us.

When we fail to understand how vastly someone's experience differs from our own or from what we assume to be true, we miss out on seeing the world as it truly is. This can be somewhat harmful to us in our day-to-day lives. We may not connect with people and not necessarily even know why. However, as therapists, this same issue can profoundly impact our work. At our best, as therapists, we are connecting with people in ways that assist them in transforming their lives. We are the person they can tell their deepest darkest secrets to without judgment. We are the person that sees them when no one else does. We are the person who understands them enough that they can understand themselves. At our worst, we have a tremendous power to make people feel worse about situations where they have no power; we can reinforce debilitating guilt and be the source of crippling negative "self talk."

We have a family friend who tells me the same story whenever it is referenced that I am a therapist. She talks about being in therapy years ago and saying to her therapist that various people did not like her and listed all of the reasons. After an unusually long rant, the therapist looked at her and said, "Well I don't like you either." This was obviously not a good therapist who possibly misunderstood experiential therapy. However, it's not about the therapist; it is the fact that this happened over 40 years ago, and it is still the first story that comes to mind for this family friend when talking to a therapist. Needless to say, her problems with people have not improved in the years since this happened to her. She is deeply affected by this. For me, this story demonstrates how much power we have as therapists. If that power is shaped by unconscious personal judgments and biases, we can inadvertently get in our own way.

We can also cause significant harm to our clients emotionally as well as in other ways. If I decided that Velma was a bad parent, who routinely makes bad choices, she would understand that quickly. She was acutely aware that the CWS worker had a low opinion of her and would not tell her anything about the abuse she experienced from her husband. This relationship was her biggest obstacle with CWS, who had the resources to help her have him removed from the home, but Velma did not trust them. Would she trust me to advocate for her with CWS? Would she trust me to help her cope with her abusive husband? Would Velma even tell me about the abuse? She had apparently stopped talking to the previous therapist about it. As I started to explore this in my analysis of her case, her presentation of the notebook and reluctance to discuss her children in a real way made more sense.

How Can I Expect to Oppress Her, Inadvertently if I am Not Careful?

What can I do to combat that? Am I assuming that she is not capable of making good decisions? Am I talking down to her? Do I make directives without checking in for her opinion? Am I on her team even when I find it hard to relate to her? Do I understand her motivations even when I do not understand her choices? For this client, especially, it became critical to rely on her ability to make the best choices for her life. It was not hard because I genuinely believed it. She had endured a very traumatic childhood as well as abuse at the hands of many others in adulthood. She was not only in recovery for several years, but had helped her husband to do the same. She was the definition of a "survivor." She was smart in ways that I could not even understand, and I was in awe of how she persevered. I treated her like she was the expert on her life and she blossomed in my office every week. In time, she trusted me and revealed more and more of her past to me and was able to process things that were eating away at her for years. The more she disclosed to me, the more her choices made sense to me which I believe is the hallmark of genuine empathy. She started to believe in herself because I believed in her and it was a miracle to witness.

How Are the Current Presenting Problems Related to Oppression?

This question can be the trickiest one. Often we do not realize how oppression so easily impacts things that we take for granted when we belong to certain dominating groups that our clients do not belong to. When working with people in marginalized groups, this is the area where we can also do the most damage. This lack of understanding of the impacts of oppression is something I routinely encounter with clients who are seeking support as they navigate helping systems. As I stated previously, for Velma, her husband was a significant obstacle with CWS. He was completely uncooperative with CWS, and it was creating an increasingly precarious situation for her. She worried every day that she would have her children removed. We had done a lot of work around her previous experiences with CWS. When she looked back in the past, she felt she probably deserved to lose her children, and this created a sense of paralysis in her now. A part of her felt like she was paying now for deeds of the past. Velma spoke with an advocate who advised that she needed to start to create a paper trail. The advocate wanted her to call the police to document the abuse, but she was adamant that she would not involve them under any circumstances. She was routinely stuck at this point, and I wanted to help her push through.

For this client, I have to ask, what did her interactions with law enforcement look like in the past? What did her interactions with the justice system and CWS look like in the past? How can I address this in session? Something that I learned a long time ago without even realizing it is that when you are in an oppressed group, part of that oppression is getting the message that you are not supposed to talk about it. So if you are in a dominating group and your client is in a marginalized group, your client is very aware of that, even if you are not. I have never had the experience of being investigated by CWS, and I am not a parent. I cannot possibly understand the level of fear involved in the threat of having your children taken out of your care and placed with strangers. This client and I are both women of color, but we have had very different experiences of the world. I might experience some routine stereotyping by law enforcement, but her experiences on the streets when her partner prostituted her would be very different.

So with Velma, it was incredibly important to address how she was likely being mistreated by CWS considering her race and her history. I also need to show her that I understood she could not control whether her husband complied with CWS. I also needed to respect her choice not to disclose the domestic violence to the police or CWS. This is probably the most controversial part of really understanding how oppression works. Very often, African American women have trouble being taken seriously about domestic violence for two reasons that I have observed. The first cause I often encounter is the concept of "strong Black woman." Tamara Winfrey Harris (2014) writes,

We are the fighters. We are the women who don't take shit from no man.

We are the women with the sharp tongues and hands firmly on hips. We are the ride-or-die women. We are the women who have, like Sojourner Truth, "plowed and planted and gathered into barns and no man could head us." We are the sassy chicks. We are the mothers who make a way out of no way. On TV, we are the no-nonsense police chiefs and judges. We are the First Ladies with the impressive guns. Strong. Black. Woman.

Calling Black women strong is often said to be a compliment. However, it also erases the victimization of Black women.

So in addition to these often unconscious assumptions, which adversely impact their mental health, we also fail these women for a second reason. We dismiss them as victims if they refuse to call the police. It becomes even more complicated because of Velma's past. She has an even more complicated history with the police. Once I looked at Velma this way, it made a lot of sense to me that she would not call the law enforcement. I needed to make it clear to her that I understood that she likely had good reasons for her choice. Sure enough a few months into our work when the therapeutic connection was stable, I brought up in a session that she must have had experiences with the police, and she responded immediately. She told me stories that horrified me about the way she and the other women she was being prostituted with were treated by the police. She thanked me for believing her and taking her seriously. It was the beginning of her disclosing so many things that she had never worked on in therapy with other therapists. Eventually, we worked together to have her abusive husband removed from the home. I do not believe she would have been able to do the necessary work to get him out of the house if we had not spent months focusing on the domestic violence in her therapy. Since his lack of cooperation was her biggest obstacle with CWS, the case was finally closed.

Clinical Supervision

In supervision, I use the framework to remind therapists how the problems their clients bring into the room might be related to oppression. This can be tricky because I am doing the work with the client and with the clinician. I encourage the clinicians to do the same exploration that I do on myself with these cases.

Tony

During supervision with one of my clinicians, we were discussing how his client presented with consistently low self-esteem, depression, and anxiety for no concrete reason that they could uncover in therapy. He had been seeing the client for about a year and a half. Tony had come to therapy for suicidal thoughts that he had been experiencing for 2 years. He was a college student and doing well in a competitive school. The client had friends and an active social life. He reported a somewhat distant, but loving, relationship with his family. He reported having some mild anxiety, but nothing else significant until 2 years ago during a challenging time in school. He had originally started in a pre-law program, but found it to be too difficult and changed to a less demanding program. He was doing very well since he changed his area of study, but he seemed to be very fixated on how his struggle in the pre-law program was evidence of him not being good enough. They had discussed several things in session, and it continued to come back to the client feeling like he just was not good enough. The therapist was confused. I asked the clinician how oppression impacted this case.

Tony is a 20-year-old, straight, cisgendered Hispanic male. His parents had emigrated from Mexico when he was 4 years old to give him and his siblings "a better life." Tony was in school on a scholarship because of his family's low income. From an oppression standpoint, he was an immigrant and of low income. I asked the therapist to think about some of the stereotypes our culture connects to those labels.

1. *What are the common stereotypes about each of the groups that the client falls into?*

   It did not take long to come up with some of the negative stereotypes floating around in our culture about immigrants (specifically from Mexico, being said by presidential candidates as I am writing this). These stereotypes are important because they give us information about how our clients experience people in their daily lives and the messages they are likely internalizing about themselves. In a client with inexplicable low self-esteem, looking at that the cultural messages he might be absorbing is helpful. It is also a good reminder for the therapist about the thoughts that he might have without realizing it. Do you make assumptions about him? Do you think he is lazy? Do you think he should just try harder? Do you wonder if his family is here legally? These are all questions that I encouraged the therapist to explore when he thinks about this client and how to approach the sessions.

2. *What are the dynamics between us because of oppression?*

   In this case, the therapist and the client are both straight cisgendered men. The therapist is White; the client is a person of color. The central dynamic between them is race, and the therapist needs to be aware of how his White privilege plays out in the therapeutic relationship. Does he expect you to understand or dismiss his accounts of racism? Does he expect you to understand his experience as an immigrant? What is it like for Tony to see people enthusiastically calling for a wall to be built to keep people coming here from Mexico? Does he worry that you see him the way others might?

3. How can I expect to oppress him inadvertently if I am not careful?

   As a person of color, the client likely experiences people with privilege not understanding how much race impacts him. The therapist, in this case, needs to bring this conversation into the room, especially because of how that oppression could be very connected to how the client feels about himself. Do you make it okay to talk about race? Do you acknowledge the differences in your experiences?

4. How are the current presenting problems related to oppression?

   Once the therapist was able to reframe how he saw the client's problem, he was able to talk to him about race. As soon as there was space for it in the room, Tony shared the immense anxiety that he always felt about not being smart enough because he did not want to fulfill the stereotype of a "lazy Mexican." He always felt like he had to work hard and do better and earn the opportunity that his parents sacrificed so much to give to him. This created the deep well of fear that he would not be good enough. When he got to school and struggled in the pre-law program, his deepest fear came true. Maybe he was not good enough. Maybe he did not deserve the chance his parents had suffered to give to him. He had not ever found the words to verbalize this until his therapist gave him the context to explore it.

Conclusion

At the beginning of this chapter, I posed the question, how can we serve our clients if we are missing huge parts of them? The answer lies in the cases discussed here along with many others belonging to myself and the clinicians that I supervise. These are people who have experienced transformations that I do not think would have been possible with therapists who did not understand how oppression impacted their lives and their identities.

So much of our work as therapists is about our work as people. Understanding the psychology of our clients is about understanding ourselves and what we bring into the therapeutic relationship. How does my parent's divorce impact the work I do with couples? How does my childhood affect the work I do with parents and children? These are the things that we have to examine. However, the nature of oppression conditions us not to look at all of these factors and makes it easy for us to passively perpetuate oppression. It causes us to have huge blind spots in our understanding of the people we encounter every day. This framework does not just reshape the therapeutic lens, it clarifies it so that we can see the whole picture and do our best work.

References

Van Kerk, K. A., Smith, D., & Andrew, C. (2011). Examining our privileges and oppressions: Incorporating an intersectionality paradigm into nursing. *Nursing Inquiry, 18*(1), 29–39.

Winfrey-Harris, T (2014).Winfrey-Harris, T (2014). Precious mettle: The myth of the strong black woman. *Bitch Magazine, 63*. Retrieved from https://bitchmedia.org/article/precious-mettle-myth-strong-black-woman.

Expanding Conversations About Cultural Responsiveness in Supervision

Shruti Singh Poulsen

Even before I became a couple and family therapist, supervisor, and scholar, my life experiences had led me to be acutely aware of context and its impact on me and the people and systems around me. Systemic and contextual conceptualization is deeply embedded in my values, beliefs, and philosophy of life and clinical work. I am a woman of color, born in India, having lived and grown up in a variety of countries before finally immigrating to the United States. I consider myself to have multiple, complex, overlapping identities because of my immigration experience, my experiences of being in an interracial intimate relationship, and my professional experiences as a systemic therapist and supervisor. It is thus no surprise (at least to me!) that, as a systemic supervisor, the concepts of cultural safety and responsiveness in clinical work with our clients and supervisees are connected and imperative, and that I rely heavily on context- and ecological-focused methods in both my therapy and supervision work. Additionally, because I am a person of multiple experiences and identities, I find integrative, holistic approaches to supervision valuable in understanding and addressing the complex issues that supervisees and their clients' experience. Understanding the dynamic nature of therapists' and clients' lives and their cultural realities is important to the therapeutic and supervision process. I present my approach for using systemic clinical tools to support a framework of cultural responsiveness in supervision, which can then translate to cultural safety in supervision, and ultimately, cultural responsiveness and safety in a therapist's work with their clients.

As a developing couple and family therapist, and later supervisor, I often encountered the edict that I needed to have expertise with one specific model to work with clients and supervisees. While I do agree that having extensive base knowledge and

S.S. Poulsen (✉)
School of Education and Human Development, University of Colorado Denver, Denver, CO, USA
e-mail: shruti.poulsen@ucdenver.edu

R. Allan, S.S. Poulsen (eds.), *Creating Cultural Safety in Couple and Family Therapy*, AFTA SpringerBriefs in Family Therapy,
DOI 10.1007/978-3-319-64617-6_3

experience in a particular therapy model is useful as a place to start and then expand to include other models, I think this can also limit our work and our ability to connect at deeper levels with our clients and supervisees. Given our own experiences as a supervisee, we may go into our supervision work with a similar approach, working with our supervisees to develop expertise and in-depth knowledge of a particular model (often our own model of choice!) with the assumption that one model will have the capacity to be applied to many, if not most, client populations and situations (Watkins, 2016). Unfortunately, this singular approach to supervision may also be detrimental to supervisees' development of cultural responsiveness that can expand cross-cultural conversations with clients and can be transformative for both client and therapist. Culturally responsive therapy and supervision support openness and space for cross-cultural conversations and understanding, and thus, also supports a supervision environment of cultural safety. When I, as the supervisor role model, demonstrate in my supervision cultural responsiveness towards supervisees and their clients, I help create a sense of emotional space, openness, and respectful curiosity to fully understand the cultural and contextual experiences of my supervisees and their clients. This, I believe, enhances a sense of cultural safety in supervision, which then also impacts the cultural safety of my supervisee's work with their clients.

In this chapter, I will illustrate how I use the common factors lens (Sprenkle, Davis, & Lebow, 2009), combined with foundational couple and family therapy techniques such as the genogram and cultural genogram (Hardy & Laszloffy, 1995) and the post-modern M.E.C.A framework (Falicov, 1995, 2007). I believe that integrating the common factors lens with the genogram and MECA can promote cultivation of and expand culturally responsive conversations for supervisees in the supervision process as well as with clients in the therapy setting. Given that attunement to client and therapist factors is considered the hallmark of effective therapy models, clinical tools such as the Cultural Genogram and Falicov's multidimensional, ecosystemic, comparative approach (MECA) can be used in clinical supervision to understand the lived realities of therapists and clients and their diverse social locations.

The Common Factors Lens and Supervision

Common factors are described as the "common mechanisms of change, which cut across all effective psychotherapy approaches" (Sprenkle & Blow, 2004, p. 114). These "common mechanisms of change" are variables that are associated with positive clinical outcomes. They are not specific to any particular approach; they are common across several or all approaches (Morgan & Sprenkle, 2007). The common factors approach enables an integrative and holistic approach connecting supervision and clinical practice (Hubble, Duncan, & Miller, 1999; Sprenkle, Davis, & Lebow, 2009; Watkins, 2016).

In establishing goals for the supervision process, the majority of my supervisees articulate that they want to better understand and develop their therapy's theoretical and practice orientation. They also want to be well-versed in models of therapy that are culturally responsive and culturally sensitive. Trainees and supervisees often feel overwhelmed by the myriad of systemic and individual psychotherapy approaches and models that they are expected to learn and maybe even master across the course of their training (Sprenkle, Davis, & Lebow, 2009). This is an impossible expectation of supervisees and one that may stymie their development as clinicians, and in particular, as systemic and culturally responsive clinicians. There are a number of ways to implement a common factors lens in supervision (Lampropoulos, 2016; Morgan & Sprenkle, 2007; Watkins, 2016). The primary way in which I apply the common factors lens in supervision is in assisting supervisees with their own development of theoretical and practice skills. I also apply the common factors lens in helping supervisees to determine their own methods of clinical practice that can be more integrative and considered their "best practices."

When I utilize the common factors lens in my supervision practices, I emphasize the integrative nature of many of the systemic models, and therefore, also point out the practices common across models that have been shown to be effective in client change processes. There are also common factors that are specific to systemic models which are important to pay attention to regardless of which model a supervisee is using—relational conceptualization, managing relational patterns, and expanded treatment systems and relational alliance (Lampropoulos, 2016; Sprenkle, Davis, & Lebow, 2009). In my practice of supervision, highlighting the importance of common practices across models has led to supervisees' deeper understanding and more flexible approach to systemic therapy that supports cross-cultural responsiveness.

Therapy trainees and supervisees often easily grasp the concepts of therapeutic alliance and the importance of generating hope and expectancy in the therapy process. "Of course," they say easily and quickly, "it is critical that we use models, techniques, and processes that engender a strong and safe therapeutic alliance, that we use models and techniques that generate a sense of hopefulness and expectation of positive outcomes in our clients!" Most trainees and supervisees "get it" when it comes to the importance of learning and using models and techniques that promote the therapeutic relationship and promote a therapy environment that is hopeful. As a supervisor, it is relatively "easy" to help supervisees see the clinical utility and importance of these two common factors. Models of therapy that have built-in methods of engaging and connecting with clients and also generating a sense of positive outcome in the process tend to be associated with positive therapeutic outcomes (Sprenkle, Davis, & Lebow, 2009).

In my supervision experience, the other two common factors, therapist characteristics and client variables, seem to be more challenging for supervisees to grasp, understand, and access. In particular, supervisees are often unable to articulate what, if anything, they are implementing or doing in therapy that helps them access these variables, and thus, adapt their clinical practices in ways that better attune to clients' needs and in particular to their clients' cultural contexts. As much as therapeutic alliance and generating hope in therapy have been demonstrated to be related to positive therapeutic outcome, understanding and attending to therapist characteristics and client variables are equally critical in regard to ethical clinical practice and positive therapeutic outcomes (Sprenkle, Davis, & Lebow, 2009). My supervision practices tend to highlight the importance, especially in terms of cross-cultural responsiveness, of the need for supervisees to integrate into their practice models and techniques that honor the exploration and understanding of both client and therapist cultural contexts.

Cultural Responsiveness, Supervision, and Common Factors

Clinical supervision that attends to cultural safety is also culturally responsive to both therapist and clients. This entails therapists being involved and engaging as learners are continuously interacting with culture and context as integral to their work, self-of-therapist work as well as their work with clients. In my experience of training and supervision, supervisees often express concern that they must first establish a therapeutic alliance with their client before they can proceed to "getting to know" their client "better" and engage in deeper cultural explorations. Supervisees also are often able to articulate that they want their clients to feel safe and hopeful about the therapy process before they can present them with more challenging questions and explorations that may be perceived as "intrusive" by clients—often these "more challenging questions and explorations" have to do with a better understanding of their clients' cultural and social contexts. As a supervisor, I explicitly work with my supervisees to see that cultural safety and responsiveness emerge from the very beginning of their clinical work with clients; the therapeutic alliance is supported and grows from the therapist's willingness to explicitly open the therapy setting to challenging questions and explorations from the very beginning of the process.

According to Falender, Shafranske, and Falicov (2014b), self-assessment and difficult conversations are integral components of culturally responsive clinical work and culturally responsive supervision. The question I often pose to my supervisees is what do they propose to do or how do they propose to establish this sense of safety of therapeutic alliance and relationship with their client? Additionally, I pose the possibility that it is these very same "more challenging questions and explorations" that might be the very mechanism by which safety, alliance, and hopefulness about the process are imparted. In particular, I highlight that working with culturally diverse clients may actually require that we get to these challenging, possibly intrusive explorations much sooner in the therapy process in order to impart the clear message that these areas of explorations are not forbidden, taboo, or extraneous; that they matter critically to the therapist's ability to provide a safe and open environment in which a client can engage in their change process (Falender et al., 2014a).

Raising supervisees' attention to clients' multicultural identities and lives is an important part of clinical supervision; with this increased attention comes the ability to be flexible and adapt therapy so that it is attuned to clients' needs and values (Falender et al., 2014b). According to Falender et al., this is accomplished by taking a "proactive, intentional stance to diversity; one that requires effort and mindful attention to the assumptions, values, and loyalties stemming from our own multicultural identities, which shape our understanding of our clients" (p. 273). Using a common factors lens to assess the effectiveness and cross-cultural responsiveness of various systemic models and techniques, I often propose supervisees to regularly incorporate two foundational and systemically sound methods of deeper cultural and contextual exploration with clients; the genogram, and more specifically the cultural genogram, and the MECA. I also utilize both these methods in my supervision and training approaches as there are parallel processes between the client-therapist relationship and the supervisee-supervisor relationship; both types of relationships can benefit from the common factors lens that the genogram, cultural genogram (Hardy & Laszloffy, 1995), and MECA (Falicov, 2014) exemplify.

Genogram and Cultural Genogram

The genogram and the cultural genogram have long been staples of systemic training processes and part of clinical assessment, treatment, and developing clinical and cultural understanding of clients' lived experiences (Hardy & Laszloffy, 1995; Lim, 2008; Keiley et al., 2002; Magnuson & Shaw, 2003; Pistole, 1997). Genograms are used not only for data gathering; the development of one's own cultural genogram can have a profound impact on a supervisee's clinical development and on their client-therapist relationships (Lim, 2008). In constructing their own and their clients' genograms, supervisees might describe their experiences as challenging, scary, intrusive, and intense; however, more often than not, they also experience construction of the genogram, with clients or their own, as transformative and effective in gaining deeper empathy and contextual understanding. Supervisees report that it is often a catalytic experience that provides them (and client) an opportunity to examine in a culturally responsive way previously held notions, assumptions, and values about oneself and the world around them. Supervisees can also make decisions about different ways of being and relating to their clients once they have more depth knowledge of their client's experiences, context, culture, and background.

Genograms and the cultural genogram have been adapted for a variety of uses in not only training setting, but also in their clinical utility; they are frequently used to enhance a supervisee's understanding of systemic concepts as well as an understanding of the self (Magnuson & Shaw, 2003). Genograms and the cultural genogram used with clients provide a framework for deepening the client-therapist trust and alliance and also engendering hope in the therapy process. When emboldened to construct a genogram with their clients, my supervisees have often reported that having the framework of the genogram process provided them with a "safe" and seemingly sanctioned structure to ask what they often perceive to be intrusive questions; ones that supervisees believe should not be asked until the therapeutic alliance is more "stable." Supervisees discover that use of the genogram and cultural genogram led to strengthening the therapeutic alliance, especially when the genogram process occurred early in the therapy setting. They report the cultural genogram to be particularly meaningful to them in challenging their own preconceived perceptions about their clients and protected them from jumping to conclusions about their clients' lived experiences and realities. Cultural "expertise" and responsiveness often seemed to be supervisees' experiences after using the genogram and the cultural genogram with clients (Pistole, 1997). Understanding client behavior in context and the complexity and diversity of client systems with the cultural responsiveness that the genogram and cultural genogram processes allow are often supervisees' experience.

The cultural genogram is a clinical process that I encourage my supervisees to engage in with their clients. Supervisees often question how to use the cultural genogram, how to organize the process, and how to depict or notate specific information (Shellenberger et al., 2007). I work with supervisees initially by having them explore their own ethnic and cultural heritages and generational family patterns by constructing their own genograms, interviewing and constructing the genograms of their fellow supervisees and trainees, and by sharing my own genogram diagrams, cultural and relational. I also describe in detail (without divulging identifying client information) my own process for using genograms in my clinical work, the response from clients that I experience, and the impact the process has on clients and the client-therapist relationship. In particular, I highlight that when I as the therapist do not share a common culture (which is more often than not!), the genogram process helps protect me, the client, and the therapy process from misunderstanding a client's culture, family, and lived experiences. Most importantly, the use of the genogram reduces the potential for clients feeling disrespected or unsafe, or for them to receive care that is not appropriate for them given their cultural experiences and context (Shellenberger et al., 2007).

I emphasize with supervisees that the genogram and cultural genogram process is congruent with common factors elements that support positive therapy outcomes, especially with culturally diverse client populations. Studies on the use of the genogram with African-Americans (McCullough-Chavis & Waites, 2016) and Asian-American clients (Lim & Nakamoto, 2008) demonstrate that the use of the cultural genogram and the genogram is effective in rapport and trust building (therapeutic alliance), particularly with client populations that historically have not felt at ease with psychotherapy. Lim and Nakamoto (2008) emphasize that the use of the genogram was found to be culturally resonant with Asian cultures, that the genogram process honored diversity, felt congruent to cultural values and experiences, and provided a context in which clients could share and explore areas of their lived experiences that might not be culturally sanctioned in other settings.

Currently, many therapy and counseling training institutions emphasize and promote post-modern sensibilities and sensitivities to issues of power, privilege, oppression, and social location as important in socially just clinical practice (Kosutic et al., 2009). While I have not formally supervised my supervisees to adapt their genograms and cultural genograms to focus on critical consciousness (Kosutic et al., 2009), I do highlight how the genogram and cultural genogram process is very much a part of socially just and culturally responsive practice. A benefit to the use of variations of the basic of the genogram process (e.g., critical genogram) is that it can help therapists expand the conceptualizations of relational dynamics to include contextual forces such as power dynamics, "isms" such as racism, sexism, classism, and other forms of oppression (Kosutic et al., 2009). Kosutic et al. developed an adaption to the traditional genogram that specifically explores, highlights, and depicts visible power differentials within and between groups and that assesses the impact of these dynamics on individuals and family systems. The authors labeled this type of genogram the "CritG" and they report this genogram allows for not only heightening therapist and client awareness of intersecting forms of oppression, but also for combating oppressive experiences. The authors refer to this as a critical consciousness genogram that allows for more socially just clinical practices in systemic therapy that can help therapists steer clear of behaviors that could be damaging to the client-therapist relationship (Kosutic et al., 2009).

Finally, the genogram technique of data collection and exploration is one that meets all the parameters of good ("best") clinical practice; i.e., a common factors approach. Genograms allow for an expanded understanding of clients' lived experiences, cultural contexts, and familial and relational contexts; thus, even the most "barebones" genogram can often provide a great deal of insight and information regarding the lives and contexts of our clients, of what they are experiencing the other 6 days and 23 h that they are not in one's therapy office. It is an invaluable tool in obtaining a rich, in-depth understanding of client factors, characteristics, and experiences.

In terms of therapist characteristics, the genogram process whether utilized as a clinical tool or a supervision and training tool provides therapists with a remarkable experience in understanding themselves, their own values and beliefs, their own cultural and familial experiences, and how these may help or hinder the therapeutic process. I make the case to my supervisees that constructing the genogram for themselves and their clients results in much greater and deeper therapeutic alliance and connection between therapist and client. Clients feel heard, understood, validated, and respected when provided with the space and structure of a genogram and cultural genogram. The process can also engender a great sense of hopefulness and expectation of a positive outcome when clients and supervisees can visualize themselves as part of something bigger, that they are not alone, and that there are indeed important and legitimate contexts for their experiences.

Multidimensional, Ecosystemic, Comparative Approach

In my continued attempts to utilize a common factors approach to therapy and supervision, I have more recently begun to incorporate the multidimensional, ecosystemic, comparative approach (Falicov, 1995; MECA) in my supervision practices as well. Like the genogram and cultural genogram, MECA resonates with the tenets of a common factors approach. Increasingly, I am utilizing the MECA conceptualization to support supervisees' exploration of their own contexts as well as their clients in a manner that is multidimensional, multisystemic, and takes the genogram and cultural genogram processes to another level of complexity (Falicov, 1995, 2007, 2014).

Falicov's MECA model adds a post-modern component to the foundational processes of the genogram in that it includes attunement to both client's and therapist's values, beliefs, and lived experiences (Falicov, 2014). Falicov posits that while psychotherapy training and supervision has attended to issues of therapist's self-awareness and examination, not much attention has been given to the perceptions and experiences of clients and therapists of each other's group (2014). These backgrounds and contexts are not value-free or neutral to the client-therapist relationship. In utilizing the MECA model in therapy and in supervision, Falicov underscores that therapists can make an active choice to view and integrate cultural contexts as central and critical to the therapy process. The MECA model provides clinicians a way to assess and treat culturally diverse clients, and also overtly highlights all of the cultural and systemic contexts that are part of the therapist's lived experiences as well (Falicov, 1995, 2007, 2014).

The focus of the MECA model is on exploring and making explicit, four domains for both client and therapist—ecological context, where the client system (and therapist system) lives and functions; migration and acculturation, where the client system (and therapist system) comes from and their adaptation to their current context; family organization, the client system's preferred structures for family and culture, the therapist system, and family life cycle, the diversity in developmental stages and transitions, and how they are impacted by cultural context (Falicov, 1995). Making these domains explicit allows therapists to increase their awareness of their own and their clients' social location. This increased awareness encourages curiosity, supports implementing challenging, "courageous" conversations early on in the therapeutic process and relationship, and reduces the potential for stereotyping and biases, making assumptions, jumping to conclusions too soon, and making inappropriate interventions that do not resonate for client or therapist.

Similar to how I encourage and motivate supervisees to incorporate the genogram and cultural genogram in their clinical work, I have begun to add the MECA component to the genogram and cultural genogram mapping that I ask of my supervisees. I encourage supervisees to incorporate into the genogram process the additional four dimensions attuning to and making explicit their own and their client's ecological context, migration and acculturation experiences, family organization, and family life cycle. I also explicitly share and make my own experiences of these four domains in the supervisory conversations by sharing my experiences as a woman of color, as an immigrant to the United States, as member of a large extended family, and as a middle-aged adult with young adult children starting their own intimate relationships and families. In sharing my domains and cultural context, I hope to provide my supervisees with another level of complexity and understanding to their own experiences as therapists engaged in the relationship of supervision and in their client-therapist relationship. Additionally, I highlight that when I, as the therapist, do not share a common culture with either the supervisee or their client, the MECA conceptualization promotes a level of complexity, understanding, and awareness that is critically amenable to cross-cultural responsiveness.

As with the genogram and cultural genogram process, layering the therapy and supervision process with the MECA process reduces the potential for clients feeling disrespected or unsafe or for them to receive care that is not appropriate for them given their cultural experiences and context. The MECA framework similar to the genogram and cultural genogram approach supports a multidimensional and multi-layered (the four domains adding additional complexity and depth) exploration and understanding of several systems, the client, the therapist, and the supervisor, and is one that meets the parameters of good ("best") clinical practice; i.e., a common factors approach attending to client factors/characteristics, therapist characteristics, therapeutic alliance, and generating hope and expectancy in the therapy process. Supervisees who are able to incorporate this multi-faceted approach to cultural and contextual exploration for self and client may also find that the process engenders and supports the important outcome of establishing a strong therapeutic alliance, creating a sense of safety and openness in therapy, as well as generating a sense of hopefulness and positive expectations of the therapy process.

Conclusion

A common factors lens to supervision and supporting supervisees' use of culturally responsive systemic tools such as the genogram and cultural genogram and the MECA model can enhance the overall cultural responsiveness of therapists and supervisors in their personal, clinical, and supervision work, and thus, also support a supervision environment of cultural safety. When working with clients and our understanding of diversity in the intersections of sociocultural contexts of their lives, integrative approaches such as the common factors approach are demonstrated to have the flexibility and adaptability to more fully and sensitively meet client needs. While no one model of therapy or specific therapy techniques meets the needs of all clients, the common factor elements found in approaches such as the genogram and cultural genogram, and the MECA model, strengthens the cultural responsiveness of these approaches. Supervisors might consider to actively encourage and support supervisees to use these lenses and conceptualizations within the context of the common factors lens (client variables, therapist characteristics, therapeutic alliance, and hope/expectancy) in order to support the cultural competency and skills of their supervisees.

References

Falicov, C. J. (1995). Training to think culturally: A multidimensional comparative framework. *Family Process, 34*, 373–388. doi:10.1111/j.1545-5300.1995.00373.x

Falicov, C. J. (2007). Working with transnational immigrants: Expanding meanings of family, community, and culture. *Family Process, 46*, 157–171. doi:10.1111/j.1545-5300.2007.00201.x

Falicov, C. J. (2014). Psychotherapy & supervision as cultural encounters: The multidimensional ecological comparative approach framework. In C. A. Falender, E. P. Shafranske, & C. J. Falicov (Eds.), *Multiculturalism and diversity in clinical supervision: A competency-based approach* (pp. 29–58). New York, NY: Guilford Press.

Falender, C. A., Shafranske, E. P., & Falicov, C. J. (2014a). Diversity & multiculturalism in supervision. In C. A. Falender, E. P. Shafranske, & C. J. Falicov (Eds.), *Multiculturalism and diversity in clinical supervision: A competency-based approach* (pp. 3–28). New York, NY: Guilford Press.

Falender, C. A., Shafranske, E. P., & Falicov, C. J. (2014b). Reflective practice: Culture in self & other. In C. A. Falender, E. P. Shafranske, & C. J. Falicov (Eds.), *Multiculturalism and diversity in clinical supervision: A competency-based approach* (pp. 273–281). New York, NY: Guilford Press.

Hardy, K. V., & Laszloffy, T. A. (1995). The cultural genogram: Key to training culturally competent family therapists. *Journal of Marital & Family Therapy, 21*, 227–237. doi:10.1111/j.1752-0606.1995.tb00158.x

Hubble, M. A., Duncan, B. L., & Miller, S. D. (1999). *The heart & soul of change: What works in therapy*. Washington, DC: American Psychological Association.

Keiley, M. K., Dolbin, M., Hill, J., Karuppaswamy, N., Liu, T., Natrajan, R., et al. (2002). The cultural genogram: Experiences from within a marriage and family therapy training program. *Journal of Marital and Family Therapy, 28*, 165–178. doi:10.1111/j.1752-0606.2002.tb00354.x

Kosutic, I., Garcia, M., Graves, T., Barnett, F., Hall, J., Haley, E., et al. (2009). The critical genogram: A tool for promoting critical consciousness. *Journal of Feminist Family Therapy, 21*, 151–176. doi:10.1080/08952830903079037

Lampropoulos, G. K. (2016). A common factors view of counseling supervision process. *The Clinical Supervisor, 21*, 77–95. doi:10.1300/J001v21n01_06

Lim, S. L. (2008). Transformative aspects of genogram work: Perceptions & experiences of graduate students in a counseling training program. *The Family Journal, 16*, 35–42. doi:10.1177/1066480707309321

Lim, S. L., & Nakamoto, T. (2008). Genograms: Use in therapy with Asian families with diverse cultural heritages. *Contemporary Family Therapy, 30*, 199–219. doi:10.1007/s10591-008-9070-6

Magnuson, S., & Shaw, H. E. (2003). Adaptations of the multifaceted genogram in counseling, training, & supervision. *The Family Journal, 11*, 45–54. doi:10.1177/1066480702238472

McCullough-Chavis, A., & Waites, C. (2016). Genograms with African American families: Considering cultural context. *Journal of Family Social Work, 8*, 1–19. doi:10.1300/J039v08n02_01

Morgan, M. M., & Sprenkle, D. H. (2007). Toward a common-factors approach to supervision. *Journal of Marital & Family Therapy, 33*, 1–17. doi:10.1111/j.1752-0606.2007.00001.x

Pistole, M. C. (1997). Using the genogram to teach systems thinking. *The Family Journal, 5*, 337–341. doi:10.1177/1066480797054012

Shellenberger, S., Dent, M. M., Davis-Smith, M., Seale, J. P., Weintraut, R., & Wright, T. (2007). Cultural genogram: A tool for teaching & practice. *Families, Systems, & Health, 25*, 367–381. doi:10.1037/1091-7527.25.4.367

Sprenkle, D. H., & Blow, A. J. (2004). Common factors and our sacred models. *Journal of Marital and Family Therapy, 30*, 113–129. doi:10.1111/j.1752-0606.2004.tb01228.x

Sprenkle, D. H., Davis, S. D., & Lebow, J. L. (2009). *Common factors in couple & family therapy: The overlooked foundation for effective practice*. New York, NY: Guilford Press.

Watkins, C. E., Jr. (2016). Convergence in psychotherapy supervision: A common factors, common processes, common practices perspective. *Journal of Psychotherapy Integration*, 1–12. doi:10.1037/int0000040

When Dominant Culture Values Meet Diverse Clinical Settings: Perspectives from an African American Supervisor

Norma Scarborough

Clinical supervision becomes more complex when interns and trainees provide therapy to people from significantly different cultural and ethnic backgrounds (Sue & Sue, 2003, p. 267). Each culture and ethnicity has created its own view of therapy and that view often does not match dominant culture definitions for solving human dilemmas. Another level of complexity is added when the cultural backgrounds of trainees and interns are different than their supervisors. When such differences exist, there may be very little intersection between worldviews. While there has been some attention given to supervisors training supervisees from different ethnicities and cultures (Gardner, 2002; McDowell, 2004; Weiling & Marshall, 1999), very little has been said about how the dominant culture trainee may be impacted by the culturally different supervisor's worldview or how these different social locations and power positions impact the supervisory relationship.

Discrepancies in worldview are particularly likely when clients are court-mandated (Pope & Kang, 2011). These clients are generally coerced into therapy by contingency plans that leave little room for refusal of treatment; they may lose their freedom or their children if they do not agree to enter into therapy (Kemps, Marcenko, Hoagwood, & Vesneski, 2009; Pope & Kang, 2011). Many mandated persons are low-income and cultural or ethnic minorities who do not necessarily accept that "talking" about your problems will be helpful (Epperson, Roberts,

Editor's Note

Norma Scarborough passed away unexpectedly early in 2016. Norma was a tireless advocate for families and family therapy, a bright light. She supervised countless family therapy interns and was an articulate voice for families of color and those marginalized by the dominant culture. Her high energy, positive spirit, and ringing laughter enriched all who knew her (and many who did not). Fortunately, her draft of this chapter was already completed. We are grateful that we can include her wisdom in this volume.

N. Scarborough, D.M.F.T. (✉)
Alliant International University, Alhambra, CA, USA
e-mail: jessica.chen@csun.edu

R. Allan, S.S. Poulsen (eds.), *Creating Cultural Safety in Couple and Family Therapy*, AFTA SpringerBriefs in Family Therapy,
DOI 10.1007/978-3-319-64617-6_4

Ivanoff, Tripodi, & Gilmer, 2013). They come from worldviews that value other ways of coping with problems (Smith, 2013). Most supervisors are likely to be from European backgrounds where talk therapy is highly valued. This may also be true of the majority of clinical supervisees. Their views of the therapeutic world may be significantly different than that of their racially and/or culturally different client (Hanna & Cordova, 2013). It is at this intersection of values and beliefs that supervisors need to be aware of the multiple realities that could significantly impact how interns and trainees deliver therapeutic interventions to culturally and ethnically diverse populations.

In my experience as an African American female, Couple and Family Therapist, and supervisor for more than 20 years, I have heard many questions and concerns voiced by supervisees that originate from differences in worldview. It is from this social location that I share perspectives drawn from my experiences as a supervisor.

As I look back over many supervisory sessions, some of the values and beliefs in question were those about time and its meaning to therapy sessions; building relationship; boundaries; poverty and its impact on clinical issues; and involvement with larger systems such as the welfare system, child protective services, the immigration system, the probation system, the police system, and the educational system, anyone of which could influence therapeutic issues. In addition, there are ethical issues about parenting and discipline that also challenged Eurocentric worldviews of dominant culture trainees and interns. Finally, there is the issue of power distribution between supervisor and supervisee. The importance of this distribution became important when trainees were asked to follow my instructions when those instructions were different from those of their dominant culture practicum instructors.

Time

In the world of the dominant culture clinician, time is not only very important, but also highly valued. It can determine how financially successful you are, as it allows you to see many clients in a day. Time is often interpreted by some trainees/interns as a way to measure the commitment of the client to therapy. This worldview about time is one that does not necessarily intersect with other cultures or the needs of clients from diverse populations. European culture believes that "time is money," "time waits for no man," and that time can be "wasted," all of which speak of the importance of time to the dominant culture. Many other cultures do not experience time as "money," but rather see it as something they have for their use (Sue & Sue, 2000, p. 269). One such miscommunication around time occurred when one trainee was seeing a Latina mother who was given an appointment from 10 am to 11 am. She arrived at the session 40 min late, still expecting to have time to meet. When the supervisee from a different worldview reported this behavior to the supervisor from a Eurocentric worldview, the mother was seen as disinterested and assessed "a resistant client." As a minority supervisor, my understanding of time was supportive of the client.

Trainees have been surprised when I have advised them to be more relaxed about time and discuss its meaning with their clients rather than make assumptions about what their client's use of time means. One trainee's response to my directions was: "But Dr. Scarborough isn't the client acting irresponsibly? Aren't I neglecting to set limits when I accept her being late?" The supervisee was encouraged to discuss the situation with the client and find out what meanings the client attached to the time rather than assume that the same understanding of time used by the supervisee was also used by the client. By having the discussion with the client, the supervisee was able to discover that the Latina mom wanted to come to therapy and believed she would be able to accomplish taking her children to school, finish dinner, and still get to the appointment. Her definition of time was based on what could be accomplished and that it all could be done. It was not defined by her desire to participate in therapy. Once the trainee understood the client's meaning of time, they were able to build relationship and open space for therapeutic work to begin. The client stated that she felt the counselor was interested in her life because of the willingness to discuss the situation. The client and the therapist were able to work out a time that worked for both of them and they understood each other better.

Another issue that trainees face about time is that many of their clients will miss a session for a couple of weeks and then show up as if they had been attending regularly. Trainees are usually puzzled by this behavior and decide that the clients have no respect for the time of the trainee. As a minority supervisor, I understood that the explanation may be somewhat different than what the trainee believed. It could be as simple as the client not understanding that the trainee is only there on certain days and does not work at the site regularly. Clients are not always aware that trainees are not "working" for the agencies in which they are being seen. The client's view of the world of traineeship is different than that of the trainee and does not necessarily represent disrespect.

It is important that the trainee develop a more positive interpretation of the client's motives, otherwise there may be a decision to discontinue treatment, with serious consequences for the client. In order to prevent a premature termination, I encouraged the trainee to engage the client in an open discussion about the trainee's concerns, their schedule, and collaborate with the client to develop a solution. Although different from the dominant culture attitudes about time constraints for therapy, creative solutions may be in order. For example, bi-weekly sessions might be better managed by the client. Clients who are mandated to therapy often have other activities and programs they are required to attend. They sometimes have difficulty managing work, home, and multiple appointments. Because these clients have been ordered to keep all their scheduled appointments, they may feel that they do not have a choice about when they are required to attend. They may believe that therapy is another class that they have to take in order to meet their contingency plan. Explaining the therapeutic process and inviting a discussion about what type of schedule would work best for the client can help to build a relationship with the client that will assist in engaging them in effective therapy.

Building Therapeutic Relationships

One of the most common concerns comes up in the beginning phases of therapy, the relationship, rapport building, or joining phase. Beginning clinicians value clients opening up and letting them in on many personal issues, even when the client has not had a chance to get to know the therapist. The new trainee often becomes concerned when diverse clients do not "open up" and may interpret this behavior as "resistance." As an African American woman, I generally understand the hesitancy of a minority client to disclose information. There are many factors that contribute to taking a protective stance with any therapist. Many have experienced being treated unfairly by larger systems such as the police or child protective services. As a minority person who has seen people in similar circumstances, it is from that vantage point that I could support the trainee and encourage them to engage clients in discussions about their experiences with mental health and other systems, without labeling the client as "resistant."

From the worldview of a mandated client, being cautious with someone who has the power to influence a judge or a social worker, probation officer, or a court case is a good decision. Anyone experiencing similar circumstances would agree that taking a protective stance with therapists and other larger systems representatives is not only reasonable but imperative. A supervisor who understands the client's world would encourage the trainee to ask questions such as "who referred you?" "What is your understanding of why you are here?" "What is your understanding of what therapists do?" A client might also benefit from hearing about the trainee and their therapeutic philosophy, i.e., how they see their work and the people they serve.

One trainee met with an African American male who was approximately 23 years old. His probation officer referred the young man because he felt that the young man was secretive and would return to prison if he did not receive help. The young man presented as anxious, guarded, and only responded in monosyllabic sentences. The male trainee, a 32-year-old Caucasian, was very frustrated and thought the young man may have been a drug abuser. He had seen the young man for three sessions and did not see any "progress." When the trainee was encouraged to explore the origins of his perceptions about his client, he realized that he had no experience with that population and most of his perceptions were informed by stereotypes and biases.

Once the trainee became aware of his worldview and how it influenced his interactions with his client, the man was able to open up and be transparent. I encouraged the trainee to begin by letting his client know that the client was his focus and that other than reporting attendance, goals, and progress to the probation officer, the trainee had no further obligations and all other information would be confidential. I suggested he express interest and curiosity about how the client came to be at this place in his life. As the client began to see genuine interest rather than pressure to "tell the therapist everything," he began to share his story. This marked the beginning of their work together. When their time together was completed, the client expressed gratitude for the trainee's ability to listen without judging and deciding how the client should live his life.

The Impact of Larger Systems

Low income may be the number one indicator of how many community systems will be involved in a client's life. In the legal system, the foster care system and the remedial education system minorities are overrepresented (Alexander, 2012; Smith, 2013). Clients who have to navigate circumstances created by not having enough money to meet basic needs often find themselves under the scrutiny of larger systems. The societal narrative about "poverty" is that it is the fault of the individual if they have limited income (Smith, 2013). Trainees from the dominant culture are often unaware of the realities of living with few economic resources. Circumstances like getting to appointments on time, not taking children to the doctor when they are ill, or working three jobs to make basic ends meet may be unfamiliar to them. Some clients often have to choose between buying food and paying the utility bills or the rent, and many times will find themselves in dire situations. Clients can present with stress related to upcoming evictions, disconnection of utilities, or a serious shortage of food. There also may be need to visit a doctor.

Therapists in training often do not feel that helping clients cope with life situations is what they should be doing and will say they do not feel like they are doing "real" therapy. As a minority supervisor, I have had experience living in low socioeconomic situations and understand the impact of prejudices and biases that influence larger system interactions with low-income persons. I understand that addressing stress from living in deprived environments and helping clients locate resources is very therapeutic. Exploring feelings and patterns of behavior will be more likely to be effective when survival issues are discussed. A trainee from the dominant culture may want to examine beliefs they hold about low-income, minorities, and their own beliefs about poverty. If they do not, they may find themselves blaming the clients for situations beyond their control. That may lead to feelings of superiority in the trainee, and the dominant culture supervisor may unintentionally reinforce those feelings.

One trainee reported working with a family that was consistently late to appointments in spite of repeated discussions with the family about the importance of being on time. The family frequently was so late that the appointment had to be rescheduled. The trainee did not explore the reasons the family was having such difficulty beyond the lack of transportation, about which they were directed to work harder to find a way to the clinic, because his supervisor only instructed him to address the lateness to appointments. The clinic had a waiting list and the supervisor wanted to discharge any clients who were not consistent with their attendance.

Because of my long history of working with families undergoing multiple stressors, I recommended listening to the families' narrative about their current circumstances. If the trainee had listened for the family's narratives he would have discovered that the family was homeless because the father, Jorge (names changed), had lost his job and had not been able to pay rent for more than 6 months. Since he was undocumented, he did not feel that he could talk to anyone about the problems he was having at his job because he had to miss so much time to attend classes.

His wife did not work and was currently 4 months pregnant with their fifth child. Their four children, aged 2, 3, 4, and 6, were placed with his mother but, because of the domestic violence case, Jorge was not allowed to stay with them. His wife, Marissa, had no family in the Unites States and nowhere to stay, so she remained with him. With no income and no real resources, Jorge and Marissa did not always have the money to pay for the bus they had to take to the clinic. They were anxious and did everything they could to get to the appointments on time because they desperately wanted to have their family back together.

Some flexibility and understanding on the part of the trainee and the supervisor may have made the difference for the couple. The trainee may have been able to advocate for them with CPS and get resources such as bus tokens and maybe hotel vouchers for them, while Jorge continued to look for work. Helping the couple change their class schedules may have enabled more time to finish the classes without feeling overwhelmed. The trainee would then have had a unique opportunity to work with the couple on the domestic violence concerns and the subsequent depression, helplessness, and anger. But unfortunately none of those steps were taken, the couple stopped comings and the case was closed.

Boundaries

Trainees frequently expressed feeling intimidated if a culturally different client asked about their personal lives; they were not sure what to say. Many have been taught by their agencies not to answer personal questions under any circumstances. They will quickly change the subject or ask the client why they want to know. A simple question like, "are you married?" can create anxiety for a trainee. Rather than subscribe to Euro-normative ways of defining boundaries, as a minority supervisor, I recognized the ways that some non-dominant culture persons may attempt to engage the therapist. The trainee's response may be used to determine if they are trustworthy to receive very private information. The response may also be used to gauge the degree of friendliness or fear a trainee may have towards them.

I advised trainees to understand that asking for personal information is a way for many ethnic minorities to build a connection to the therapist. The trainee may try being transparent about feelings of discomfort about revealing personal information. An honest explanation would help the client understand the trainee's reticence and not misinterpret it as the trainee looking down on the client. Guidance by the trainee's supervisor is important, and the supervisor is encouraged to understand the motivations of ethnic or cultural groups to know something about the therapist.

New clinicians may need to understand that since boundaries for therapy are defined by European values, other ethnicities may not have the same definition. My experience has been that when clients ask questions, they are asking if the therapist is comfortable enough with the client to answer. It is often a way to gage whether a therapist is prejudiced or biased. Openness about trainee's thoughts, i.e., in school we were taught not to reveal personal information or say "I am not really comfortable talking about myself in a session that I should use to find out more about your needs," could be helpful in helping clients relax. They will be able to determine that the trainee does not have disdain for them and their decision not to answer personal questions is not because the trainee thinks that the client is inferior. Trainees may also be encouraged to share personal experiences and emotions as a way to build two-way relationship (Elias-Juarez & Knudson-Martin, 2016).

Parenting and Discipline

There are many styles of parenting and many minorities have their own unique ways of raising and disciplining children. The issues around parenting arise when one culture defines good parenting and appropriate discipline. Embedded in the definition is also the understanding of what constitutes bad parenting. Corporal punishment is not acceptable in the minds of most therapists, even though there are many ethnic groups that use it. The use of corporal punishment is often confused with child abuse. Child abuse implies deliberate intention to harm a child. Parents who use corporal punishment are using it to teach their children right from wrong. Spanking in and of itself is not child abuse. Leaving injuries on a child as a result of spanking is reportable. Rather than treating parents as child abusers, working with them to find alternative disciplines is appropriate for cultures that believe in corporal punishments.

As a minority supervisor, I would recommend talking with the parent if a remark is made about "whipping" their child to determine discipline habits. If such a conversation occurs, a trainee may discover that a mother was embarrassed by her child's behavior and did not want the trainee to think that she could not control her child. It is very possible that a client would never injure her child and often threatened but never followed through. A trainee may discuss the frustration of parenting a young child and work on ways to parent children that would address both the needs of the child and the concerns of the parents. It is an opportunity to build relationship and trust needed to bring about effective change.

Power Distribution in Supervision

The concept of privilege cannot be omitted when discussing the location of power in supervisory relationships. I initially believed that an education in the field would place me on equal footing with my peers. I did not experience myself as inferior or as having inadequate ability. However, when working with dominant culture supervisees, I often found that my concepts and recommendations were challenged. I would be asked if there were any articles or readings that would back up what I was telling them or they would check with their practicum instructors and tell me how the instructor disagreed with what I said.

Either way, I felt my trainees did not trust what I was teaching and I was not sure, at first, why. I began to understand what W.E.B. Du Bois meant when he asked "how does it feel to be the problem" (Du Bois, 1903). One incident in particular was very disheartening. In a foster family agency setting, I was supervising two dominant culture trainees to whom I had explained the differences and expectations of in-home work. I invited them to several meetings at the agency *before* they signed the agreement to start their practicum training. After several weeks of observing and working with others who were involved, they decided that they wanted to start. Initially, they reported that they were fine with the work. In supervision, I challenged several perceptions about foster parents and the trainees' role with them. Apparently, they were unhappy and spoke to their clinical training coordinator who was not a clinician. The coordinator called me and accused me of working outside my scope of practice. I explained to her what I was doing and why her accusations were not correct. She then said that I should have told the trainees what they would be doing and that I had mislead them and she was therefore pulling them out of their agreements. I was shocked that she had not considered that I was (1) competent and (2) that I would not mislead trainees. I did not feel that I had been given the benefit of a doubt and felt very strongly that it was the result of stereotypical worldview of African Americans that influenced the coordinator.

At first, it did not occur to me that culture and societal narratives about culture may have shaped these interactions. I was aware of power and privilege, but did not connect them to interactions with students. I felt that I had power and privilege in the relationships because of my experience in the field. Privilege in the reverse, where the trainee held the privilege in a supervisory relationship, had not been an experience that I was prepared for or initially recognized. As I had more and more experiences with dominant culture supervisees, I was forced to look at the supervisory relationship from a different perspective. I looked at the power distribution from the standpoint of differences in worldview. Many of my supervisees had never seen or been involved with an African American supervisor or professor. Their experiences with African Americans were influenced by unexplored biases, prejudices, and stereotypes. I believed that their responses to my supervision were largely from experiences that informed their worldview of African Americans. I invited supervisees to have open discussion about anything they felt comfortable discussing; I remained informative and compassionate with their anxieties and concerns about therapeutic work; and most of all I helped them discover their own potential to become excellent therapist, something that was always my goal for my supervisory journey.

Conclusion

The role of a supervisor is influenced by many factors. Minority supervisors have a worldview that influences their perspectives and informs the way in which they approach supervision. These experiences may differ from dominant culture supervisors and trainees, especially when working with minority populations with which they have shared experiences. Supervisees must challenge their own worldviews to be able to accept different ways of seeing their minority clients' clinical dilemmas and to intervene effectively. Minority/ethnic supervisors may be instrumental in preparing students and interns to see the therapeutic world from a different worldview.

References

Alexander, M. (2012). *The new Jim Crow: Mass incarceration in the age of colorblindness*. New York, NY: The New Press.

Du Bois, W. E. B. (1903). *The souls of black folk*. New York, NY: Barnes & Noble Classics.

Elias-Juarez, M. A., & Knudson-Martin, C. (2016). Cultural attunement in therapy with Mexican-heritage couples: A grounded theory analysis of client and therapist experience. *Journal of Marital and Family Therapy, 43*(1), 100–114. doi:10.1111/jmft.12183

Epperson, M. W., Roberts, L. E., Ivanoff, A., Tripodi, S. J., & Gilmer, C. N. (2013). To what extent is criminal justice content specifically addressed in MSW progress. *Journal of Social Work Education, 49*(1), 96–107.

Gardner, R. M. D. (2002). Cultural perspectives in supervision. *The Western Journal of Black Studies, 26*(2), 98–106.

Hanna, F., & Cordova, B. (2013). Multicultural counseling beyond relationship: Expanding the repertoire with techniques. *Journal of Counseling Development, 91*(3), 349–357. doi:10.1002/j.1556-6676.2013.00104.x

Kemps, S., Marcenko, M. O., Hoagwood, K., & Vesneski, W. (2009). Engaging parents in child welfare services: Bridging family needs and child welfare mandates. *Child Welfare, 88*(1), 101–126.

McDowell, T. (2004). Exploring the racial experience of therapists in training: A critical racial theory perspective. *The American Journal of Family Therapy, 32*, 305–324. doi:10.1080/01926180490454791

Pope, N. D., & Kang, B. (2011). Social work students' attitudes about working with involuntary clients. *Journal of Teaching in Social Work, 31*(4), 442–456. doi:10.1080/08841233.2011.597677

Sue, D. W., & Sue, D. (2000). Counseling the *culturally different: Theory and practice* (3rd ed.). New York: John Wiley and Sons

Sue, D. W., & Sue, D. (2003). *Counseling the culturally diverse: Theory and practice* (4th ed.). Hoboken, NJ: Wiley.

Smith, L. (2013). Counseling and poverty. In D. W. Sue & D. Sue (Eds.), *Counseling the culturally diverse: Theory and practice* (6th ed., pp. 516–526). Hoboken, NJ: Wiley.

Weiling, E., & Marshall, J. P. (1999). Cross-cultural supervision in marriage and family therapy. *Contemporary Family Therapy, 31*(3), 317–327. doi:10.1023/A:1021908331433

Safety and Social Justice in the Supervisory Relationship

Jessica ChenFeng, Marj Castronova, and Toni Zimmerman

A quotation often attributed to Maya Angelou is "People will forget what you said, people will forget what you did, but people will never forget how you made them feel." This captures our experience and what we learned in our pursuit of better understanding safety and social justice in the supervisory relationship. We wrote an introductory chapter to this topic in another volume (Zimmerman, Castronova, & ChenFeng, 2015), and rather than continuing to assume that our ideas about supervision were effective and expand on them, for this chapter we decided to engage our supervisees in dialogue to learn about their experience as our supervisees. Indeed, we found it is imperative to first build safety within the supervisory relationship, as these relational dynamics are isomorphic. In order to do this, we emphasize the importance of a mutually collaborative supervision relationship and our proposing our CARE model: (1) Connecting with supervisees through sharing backgrounds/context; (2) Appreciating privilege, power, and biases; (3) Ratifying a cultural knowledge base with cultural humility; and (4) Embracing our role as social justice agents. Each of these CARE principles is grounded in what we already know from the literature.

In each of these areas, we present formal and informal questions to foster and check in on safety and social justice within the supervisory relationship. This intentionality of engaging in a reciprocal process of checking in with thoughtful questions

J. ChenFeng (✉)
Department of Educational Psychology & Counseling, California State University Northridge, Northridge, CA, USA
e-mail: jessica.chen@csun.edu

M. Castronova
Relational Wellness Institute, Las Vegas, NV, USA

T. Zimmerman
Department of Human Development and Family Studies, Colorado State University, Fort Collins, CO, USA

R. Allan, S.S. Poulsen (eds.), *Creating Cultural Safety in Couple and Family Therapy*, AFTA SpringerBriefs in Family Therapy,
DOI 10.1007/978-3-319-64617-6_5

allows us to make adjustments accordingly. In the area of diversity, reciprocal valuing of the other is essential for creating safety to explore differences. Intention and impact are sometimes not aligned in diversity work. Therefore, checking in using the CARE model is essential. It is imperative to realize that good intentions without a commitment to issues of social justice and diversity can bring more harm unless we are frequently checking that our intentions are having a positive impact. Microaggressions can happen that are outside our awareness and opportunities can be missed where a situation felt marginalizing to supervisees. Therefore, if frequent check-ins are not conducted, it is unlikely that honest feedback from supervisees will be reported and supervisors will not have opportunities to repair and respond in a way that creates connection and growth.

All three of us are marriage and family therapy professors, supervisors, and practicing clinicians, working at universities in different states with very different contexts. Caring about and seeing through a social justice lens is at the foundation of our lives and our hope is that our supervision reflects this value. Jessica is a second-generation Taiwanese American, heterosexual, cisgender, Christian, able-bodied, married woman in her 30s. She has come a long way in understanding her experiences of marginalization and seeks to be one who advocates and empowers supervisees and clients as someone born and raised in Los Angeles. She also continues to seek accountability for her areas of privilege, particularly in raising consciousness within Asian American communities of faith. Marj is a 52 year old, heterosexual re-married woman, German/Norwegian American with one adult daughter, three adult step-daughters, and nine grandchildren. She is a deeply, devout Christian who has been saddened and discouraged by the single-mindedness of any group that creates polarization of one another and create labels of division. In her journey of coming to grips with understanding her privileges, she is passionate about being a voice that brings understanding and opens doors that should never have been closed. Toni is a heterosexual, cisgender, able-bodied, Euro-American, Caucasian, 54 year old, married woman with two adult daughters; she also identifies as first generation in terms of education, and her spirituality is central in her life, but she is not committed to or affiliated with any religion or religious organization.

In our dialogues with each other and our supervisees, we wondered "are our intentions to promote social justice and have respect for diversity central to their supervision experience with us?" As a result of asking these questions, and valuing the reciprocal process we so believe in, this chapter has been guided by their words and their experiences of us in supervision. Supervisees represented the following demographics: male and female; age, late twenties to early 40s; partnered and single; they identified as Christian from various religious backgrounds; heterosexual and gay; lower to upper middle socio-economic status. The ethnicities of the group included Puerto Rican, Brazilian, Bi-Racial, African-American, Ethiopian, Argentinian, and Caucasian. These supervisees were just completing their master level training in marriage and family therapy. They were given the opportunity in their final course to process the experience of supervision in relation to diversity. The assignment was optional and all supervisees who participated wanted their feedback shared.

Connecting with Supervisees

"I can tell she just has such a big heart, she genuinely cares for people and wants nothing but the best. I can just tell that is just the essence of who she is." (Bi-Racial Supervisee).

Relationships are at the foundation of solid supervision (Deihl & Ellis, 2009a, 2009b; Fama & Ellis, 2005; Inman, 2006). Alliance and connection between supervisor and supervisee are major predictors of satisfaction in supervision (Inman, 2006; Ladany, Ellis, & Friedlander, 1999). In order to integrate social justice and open dialogue about social location in supervision, safety needs to be experienced. How a supervisor facilitates this sense of safety for supervisees impacts the quality of the relationship (Killian, 2001).

Ways to Connect

There are activities and tools we use to connect with supervisees. One such tool is the cultural genogram (Hardy & Laszloffy, 1995, 2002). We share our cultural genograms with supervisees and offer stories of how we have navigated our own identities in clinical work. It is also a way to learn about supervisees' backgrounds. This can be done in individual supervision or in group supervision, based on the supervisee's comfort level. There is a mutual knowing of the other and feeling known by the other. Supervisors can also establish supervisory norms so that supervisees expect to talk about clients' social location and understand these in light of their own.

Supervisees' Experience of Connection

When we talked with our supervisees about what we did that led to an experience of connection and safety in the supervisory relationship, they shared three things: feeling their supervisor's authenticity and vulnerability, feeling validated by the supervisor, and witnessing their supervisor's empathy and compassion.

Supervisor authenticity and vulnerability: One supervisee shared "[My supervisor] was open about her social location and previous experiences with supervision in which supervisors were not sensitive to diversity topics. This made me feel as if I had a safe place to discuss my thoughts on how a subject of diversity may be impacting a client or me …" The supervisor initiating this process of self-disclosure around their own social location is perceived by supervisees to be authentic and vulnerable; this gives them permission to do the same and to feel safe doing so.

Another supervisee shared about the supervisor saying that "Both of us having experiences of discrimination and our own biases was a joining point." Connection in supervision also takes place when supervisors are willing to be open about their

Table 1 Check-in questions to assess for connection

What did your supervisor do that helped you feel connected in the supervisory relationship?
What conversations about your own background/social location as well supervisor's background were helpful in creating safety in the supervisory relationship?
Are there things that your supervisor modeled that supported you towards how to better work with clients who have a different background from you?
Do you wish there were things done differently, or more/less of something, to help you feel safe and connected in the supervisory relationship?

implicit biases, areas of privilege, as well as experiences of oppression and discrimination.

Validation of supervisees' experience: When supervisees were asked about their experience of safety in supervision, one common response was that of being validated, heard, and seen by the supervisor. The supervisor was able to really see the supervisee with their whole identity: "Listening and validating my experiences when I expressed myself about my background;" "She was knowledgeable and understanding of my culture and personality." We as supervisors can facilitate an experience of safety by really getting to know and understand our supervisees and their intersectional social identities. Additionally, supervisees felt safe when supervisors took time to listen and receive their perspectives: "She was open to my feedback;" "Her willingness to listen attentively to my viewpoint;" "I was actually given the time and the full attention to express myself." In order to facilitate an experience of safety in supervision, we must create space for supervisees' voices to be expressed and heard.

Witnessing supervisor's empathy and compassion: An interesting way supervisees experienced connection with supervisors is from their observations of supervisors' actions outside of the supervisory relationship. One supervisee shared "[The supervisor] gives her all in everything she does. When she was supervising a case, it ended up going way over session and she didn't care about the time, she just cared about the family getting the proper care needed." This supervisee witnessed her supervisor's care and empathy toward a family receiving therapy. Supervisees see what we say and teach in action and get a sense of who we are from interactions beyond the hour or few hours of weekly supervision. When who we are is congruent across multiple settings, supervisees feel a greater sense of trust and connection (Table 1).

Appreciating Privilege, Power, and Biases

The second part of the CARE model intentionally appreciates privilege, power, and biases. Creating and maintaining a safe relationship between supervisor and supervisee hinges on well-managed power differentials (Inman, 2006; Killian, 2001). A supervisor may be highly knowledgeable about power, but if they do not manage it in their everyday interactions with their supervisees, knowledge remains a cognitive exercise and not a lived experience. It is evident by the supervisee quotes in this section that they are attuned to the management of power differentials in all interactions with their supervisors, not just in the supervision session(s). It is critical for even the best trained supervisors in the area of diversity to embrace diversity as a life lens and not an area of competency that they turn on and off depending on the setting. This is why we are calling our first theme in this area *Role-Modeling*. It is also evident from our supervisee feedback that *Kindness* toward others by supervisors is an important demonstration of appreciating privilege, power, and biases. Many supervisees mentioned supervisors going out of their way to be kind, particularly in situations where the client or supervisee are persons who hold less privilege and experience more bias in our society (Divac & Heaphy, 2005). Kindness was associated with humility and empathy shown by the supervisors to others (Hook, Davis, Owen, Worthington, & Utsey, 2013). *Valuing Voices* was a theme the supervisees reported made a big difference in feeling safe. This was particularly true for marginalized supervisees (Nadal, Griffin, Wong, Hamit, & Rasmus, 2014; Nieto & Boyer, 2006; Pendry, 2012).

Ways to Appreciate Power, Privilege, and Bias

There are activities and tools to use to appreciate power, privilege, and bias in supervision. One such tool is GGRRAACCEESS (Burnham, Alvis Palma, & Whitehouse, 2008). Categories of marginalized persons that are most affected by bias and institutional "isms" are gender, geography, race, religion, age, abilities, class, culture, ethnicity, education, sexual orientation, and spirituality. Clarity concerning who we are referring to when we speak of less privilege and more bias is important and GGRRAACCEESS gives us an easy way to talk about it in supervision. Despite our best intentions, we tend to have hidden bias in our unconscious along the 11 dimensions. Having supervisee and supervisors take the Implicit Association Test (IAT; Greenwald, McGhee, & Schwartz, 1998) which measures our implicit biases is a helpful activity for increasing our awareness. We make judgments about people, particularly marginalized people, as an automatic brain response (Stanley, Phelps, & Banaji, 2008). Awareness of our bias, through the IAT, can identify the bias areas we most need to be attuned to. As an activity to understand how bias occurs in our brains, we suggest watching a TedTalk by Chimamanda Adichie, titled *The Danger of a Single Story.* Through the metaphor of "a single story," Adichie eloquently explains how these automatic responses happen. Using GGRRAACCEESS, the IAT, and the Single Story as metaphor can go a long way in supervision to keep power, privilege, and bias in the forefront of our work with clients and in our supervisory relationships.

Role Model

It was interesting how often supervisees referred to the supervisor's actions and comments that did not occur in a supervision session as demonstration to them of well-managed power, privilege, and bias. "My supervisor is part of an

African-Brazilian musical group, that made me love her more. We had something in common, something to link us." It meant something to this supervisee that a supervisor was interested in other cultures as part of her recreation not simply education. This conversation happened when a group of supervisees took a break from a class lecture and the supervisees and supervisor were walking together to get a cup of coffee. The supervisor was role-modeling the relational part of their relationship, creating an environment of safety to talk to demonstrate that this is part of who the supervisor is at the human level. Another way the supervisors balanced power was in terms of their interactions with their supervisees. Supervisees noted "They [supervisors] don't need to prove themselves through hierarchy and minimizing others. [My supervisor] is empowering and doesn't waste time in accolades to prove who she is." "My supervisor is very well aware of her privilege but does not have any desire to use it to her advantage." These supervisees feel assured that power will not be misused.

Another way supervisees noted how there was an appreciation for power, privilege, and biases was in their willingness to check their own biases and even adjusting them. One supervisee noted "I witnessed my supervisor checking on her own biases which made me more aware of my own biases especially, when they related to adjusting my lens. Almost like an optometrist, when they click the lenses for the patient to have clear vision, my supervisor was really great with asking questions to provoke my lenses to be adjusted for clarity." The supervisee had learned that when she was challenged by her supervisor on bias, she could trust that her supervisor was also checking her own bias as she had experienced conversations in the past where the supervisor shared her own bias and how she was working on them. Supervisors also normalized the idea that we all have biases. One supervisee noted "Biases were handled directly, not danced over or avoided. They were addressed in a way that if another supervisee brought up the bias others were able to process through the experience as well and reflect." Another supervisee noted that the supervisor was also being willing to be called out on her bias. "I feel that [my supervisor] is very humble and accepts feedback and really wants to understand what people are experiencing." Directness with a collaborative style was much appreciated by the supervisees as a way to manage power.

When supervisees who had White privilege and were having to learn to keep in check what that meant, they noted that it was helpful to see a White supervisor model this. One supervisees said, "Having similar social GGRRAACCESS as my supervisor in this situation was extremely helpful because I saw how a White woman stays aware of biases and diversity issues in her work in supervision and in cases. She was a great role model in this aspect (and many others)." Supervisors also model the idea of power, privilege, and bias by how they model balancing these three topics that are ever present in the classroom. "When she taught, she did a good job of keeping control of the room and the conversations so that no one felt left out or overshadowed." This is another example of managing power outside the supervision session as noticed by the supervisees. Supervisees were very tuned into supervisors who treated them "equally;" one supervisee noted "I feel that [my supervisor] treated us as colleagues. She never treated us like we were less than her."

Valuing Personhood

One theme that crossed all sections, but we have chosen to highlight it in the section of power, privilege, and biases, was the idea of basic kindness toward others. We have decided to call this valuing personhood. A supervisor is in a position of power by the nature of their position, but they can have more power and privilege based on their social GGRRAACCESS. When supervisees experienced their supervisors treating them as a person of value, we believe it makes a difference that should be noted. One supervisee said, "I can tell she just has such a big heart, she genuinely cares for people and wants nothing but the best. I can just tell that is just the essence of who she is." If the supervisor values the supervisee as a person, the supervisee will experience this in supervision. It is in this place of valuing others that one supervisee noted, "I felt connected because she listened and had this form of compassion that isn't easy to describe, but you can feel it. In this case, me being African-American, the lead therapist and clients Caucasian - was irrelevant. She saw human connection and drew from best practices and gave those clients the best care. It felt like I was a human and she was a human, both wanting the best for the clients." The supervisee appreciated the supervisor's ability to distinguish times to move beyond implicit bias and value human connection.

Valued Voice

Really listening to our supervisees and valuing their voices was a strong recurring theme. There is a difference between valuing the person as we just discussed and valuing the supervisee's voice. In appreciating the concepts of power privilege and biases, supervisees were tuned with supervisors who spend time listening and asking questions and asking questions of what the supervisees were seeing in the case made a difference in the idea of a valued voice. Supervisees noted valued voice in statements like: "My supervisor was respectful of my thoughts and listened to my voice and always provided a space for me to talk through cases. She also never made assumptions, only asked clarifying questions" or "My involvement was encouraged to balance the power." Supervisees were attuned to if the supervisor was interested in their thoughts, such as "My supervisor does a great job of asking what I think about a case before sharing her thoughts." When problems arose, supervisees appreciated supervisors not jumping to conclusions. "One time I made a huge mistake and instead of her assuming the worst of me, she was very understanding and wanted to see what was going on in my life and she even encouraged me." (Table 2)

Table 2 Check-in questions for power, privilege, and bias

You have learned about managing power, privilege, and bias. What are examples from any of the supervision you experienced or witnessed that you would consider positive or negative in this area?
What happened that made you feel that power was well-managed (or not) between the supervisee and supervisor?
How did you experience bias being attended to? How did your social GRRAACCESS as well as that of the supervisor (and the client's) influence what was happening?

Ratifying a Cultural Knowledge Base with Cultural Humility

"Her knowledge about different cultures inspires me to want to learn more." (Brazilian Supervisee).

Our knowledge of varying cultures is often times limited by our own experiences with various cultures and the discourses around us and we rely on our clients' stories to inform us. These typical paths to cultural awareness can limit us and leave us without realizing the implications of questions we are not asking because of our lack of knowledge. It is important to have knowledge of a wide range of cultures and cultural practices as a starting place and not solely rely on the clients to teach the therapist. Adams (1995) notes that cultural knowledge is when we are familiar with a variety of characteristics, history, values, beliefs, and behaviors of a group. It involves researching different groups and integrating personal experiences. Supervisees mentioned the importance of learning that knowledge is an ongoing journey and process. One supervisee noted, "My journey with cultural humility was modeled to me by my supervisor and I have been challenged to travel this journey."

When therapists begin to see clients from backgrounds either unfamiliar to them or different from their own supervision, they should include learning about that background in a variety of ways. We have previously highlighted various ways for supervisors to guide their supervisees to access cultural knowledge (Zimmerman et al., 2015). Adams (1995) says that cultural awareness is when we have internally changed our attitudes and values because we have developed a sensitivity and understanding. We wondered as supervisors how this happens for our supervisees and they reported the following themes as being critical to their awareness: addressing their own bias and privileges; supervisor trusting the supervisees to come to their own conclusions; modeling the cultural humility journey.

Addressing Bias and Privilege in Cultural Knowledge

Supervisees reported that they were challenged by their supervisors on a plethora of social GGRRAACCEESS, including race, sexual orientation, sexual identity, family composition, physical ability, and age. They were challenged to think differently about their own social location. One supervisee noted "I think that I have been challenged to look at my race differently and how Caucasians are generally unaware of the privilege they hold in society and how dangerous this can be if someone is unaware of this a therapist." Supervisees noted that having a safe place to explore different biases was important to their process. The also noted that the supervisor "consistently addressed our biases in every opportunity" and asked questions like "what do you think about that?" and "what made you take this path/decision?" At times, supervisees noted that the supervisor would describe "a different perspective, without explicitly mentioning bias." One supervisee noted that "Biases were handled directly, not danced over or avoided. They were addressed in a way that if another supervisee brought up the bias, others were able to process through the experience as well and reflect." Supervisees noted it was also important that their supervisor talked about their own journey of confronting bias. One supervisee shared "She was honest about her own processes around her bias and encouraged all of us to talk about ours."

In our previous chapter on supervising supervisees in experiencing diversity, we suggest that supervisees have lived experiences with cultures different than theirs via traveling, working, or volunteering in various places around the globe to see firsthand how people live and work (Zimmerman et al., 2015). When supervisees have not had experiences of global travel or are unable to travel due to their economic situation, we have proposed they read autobiographies of people or watch documentaries of different cultures. Supervisors can also be intentional in sharing their own experiences with other cultures and how it has helped them think differently. One supervisee noted "My supervisor really allowed for me to understand culture and diversity. The experience with her and how she walked through scenarios was absolutely amazing … real life application and how to foster connectedness with people in a genuine manner." The point is for supervisors to encourage their supervisees to get out of their comfort zones by getting them to go to places they generally would not go and meet people with whom they do not generally interact.

In order for supervisees to have personal encounters with many people who are different from themselves, we also suggest supervisors assist in "brokering opportunities" (Zimmerman et al., 2015). One supervisee reported this was important in confronting her own bias toward the LGBTQ community. The supervisor had arranged for her to meet a Jewish, Black, gay man who was living in a same-sex marriage and was a Christian and a worship leader at his church. Another supervisee who was born in another country and traveled the world extensively as a missionary said, "I was very intolerant to racism before, not because I have personally suffered with it but I have seen a lot with other people and that makes me very, very mad. What has changed is that now I can see that racist people may have been influenced by the discourses around them and may have had other types of influences. I can be more compassionate and try to assess their point of view and how that may have impacted them."

What is a challenge for many supervisees is the idea of everything being congruent and fitting into a nicely wrapped package. Therapists are working with clients of all different points of view, and often times, client's implicit biases are off and this can impact the therapy room. Working with supervisees to understand the idea of intersectionality can help to broaden their ability to work with contradictions.

Intersectionality may create conflicting stories for the supervisee. Crenshaw (1993) defines intersectionality as a process where various social locations, such as religion, culture, and gender, can co-construct our sense of self, thus influencing our identities, choices, and opportunities often within the voice of the dominant culture (De Reus, Few, & Blume, 2005). For instance, being gay as a Black man from a conservative religious background will be significantly different than being a White man coming out in a progressive religious culture. It is easy for our "labels" of others to create wrong conclusions as they are influenced by our implicit bias. We all have individual stories and labels can minimize stories; supervisees noted that in being more aware of others' realities, they realized that they also have a story of discrimination. When we help our supervisees to see that labels are social constructs, it challenges them to consider how their own privilege and bias might be influencing them.

Trusting Supervisees to Come to Their Own Conclusions

Having some working knowledge of a variety of cultural practices will provide the supervisee with an introduction into the culture with which her client identifies. Supervisors can work with supervisees to use this as a foundation from which to build. The supervisee can begin to ask herself questions about how this client's background might be similar and/or different from her own and begin to wonder how what she has learned matches or does not match the experience of her client. One supervisee shared how her supervisor had helped her do this, "I can hear her saying, "Did you think about it like…? So, based on their social GGRRAACCEESS, what would you think? Now, based on their social GGRRAACCEESS, what do you think?" She then asks a follow-up question and the process would be so revealing. She drew the answer out of me and showed the answer was within." Trusting supervisees to come to their own conclusions also means providing them the space to process. We have learned that this is also the case when working with supervisees who have strong values on certain social GGRRAACCEESS, so providing supervisees with contradiction of demographics through the idea of intersectionality provides them with a space to confront their own biases. One supervisee noted, "The most helpful thing she did for me was to allow me to come up with my own conclusions and understanding."

Modeling and the Cultural Humility Journey

"My journey with cultural humility was modeled to me by my supervisor and I have been challenged to travel this journey with an open mind." (Ethiopian Supervisee).

Supervisees should be reminded to have cultural humility (sometimes referred to as cultural curiosity) with their clients. Cultural humility has been defined as "the ability to maintain an interpersonal stance that is other-oriented (or open to the other) in relation to aspects of cultural identity that are most important to the client" (Hook et al., 2013, p. 354). In learning to maintain this other-oriented stance, it is helpful for the supervisor to provide the supervisees with experiences where they can explore their own bias and create an environment of humility and respect for differing perspectives. One supervisee said that his supervisor had provided a "safe place to try on different perspectives and explore biases. This meant the teacher and the rest of the supervisees were 'accepting and strong enough to hear differing perspectives without reacting negatively, but instead constructively.'"

When supervisees have some knowledge of their client's culture and are able to stay humble and curious about the actual lived experiences, clients are honored and respected. It means that even when cultural differences threaten to weaken the therapeutic alliance, the therapist still expresses respect and does not assume competency based on prior knowledge (Hook et al. 2013). Teaching supervisees cultural humility begins with the supervisor modeling this. Supervisors need to take the time to hear their supervisees. Each supervisee has a unique story of diversity. In listening to the supervisees' story, the supervisor is also modeling they are always in a state of learning about others. One supervisee shared that "By giving us the time to express ourselves, she gave importance to our stories. It made me feel as if she really wanted to get to know me as a person." It also means that the supervisor is keeping cultural humility at the forefront in supervision. One supervisee noted, "Seeing it continually modeled by different supervisors and despite each having different biases and opinions, we can all connect will in a therapeutic training environment."

In working with supervisees, supervisors may want to consider using the Cultural Humility Scale (CHS; Hook et al., 2013), a measure that has clients share their perception of their therapist's cultural humility. The higher the client reported perception of the therapist's cultural humility, the stronger the alliance in the therapy process (Hook et al., 2013). In addition, there was a large effect size for the client's improvement in therapy explained by the mediated effect of cultural humility through the working alliance. Supervisors can use the CHS as a way to assess supervisees with regard to cultural humility and the effect it is having on the working alliance and clients' improvement (Table 3).

Embracing Our Roles as Social Justice Advocates

"MFT work is social justice work because we are engaged in the process of change in relationships where the balance of power might be unequal. We have opportunities to engage in social justice work through our work." (Ethiopian Supervisee).

Anytime we step into the role of brokering equality in relationships and seeking justice, we are doing the work of social justice. Repeatedly, throughout our feedback from supervisees was the theme of their supervisors being passionate about diversity and social justice. Supervisors need to help supervisees identify situations where

Table 3 Check-in questions for cultural knowledge base and humility

What client population or social location have you been challenged to think about differently?
What was helpful about the way your supervisor facilitated growth for you about this population?
How would you describe your journey with cultural humility? How has this been helpful in helping you connect with supervisor and clients?

social justice issues are present. In our CARE Model, we come from a place of assuming there are always issues of power, privilege, and biases present. The reason we don't identify them in our cases is because we aren't looking for them or asking potential questions that will bring them to the surface. A supervisee noted "My supervisor being the voice of the "other" was helpful. She would help me see from the "other" perspective and challenged me to be empathetic. She would also provide personal stories that allowed me to see how much damage could be done when as therapists we remain indifferent to things that affect the lives of our clients." The idea of the "other" is to ask the question about the perspectives of all the clients in the therapy room as well as any key stakeholders who may be involved with the case. These questions also include intentionally asking how their lives might be impacted by issues of power, privilege, and bias. For example, one supervisee who worked with young unwed mothers who had been disenfranchised by their families noted that her supervisor "being the voice of the [young mothers] was helpful. She would help me see from their perspective and challenge me to be empathetic. She would also provide personal stories that allowed me to see how much damage could be done when as therapists we remain indifferent to the things that affect the lives of our client." The supervisor would ask questions about what it would be like for a teen to be completely abandoned by family and friends and to have no support and her only resource was to be in a group home. The supervisor at times may also ask hypothetical questions about why the teen's parents aren't involved or why they may not have enough resources for another mouth to feed and this may have been the only option. Being intentional to ask about the voice of the "other" in therapy is to bring additional perspectives into the supervisee's understanding of the case.

It is not enough to address diversity issues in our supervision work with our supervisees in the therapy room. We must also work with them to intervene wherever and whenever possible outside the therapy room, reminding our supervisees that their direct interventions on the behavior of their clients need to be done within legal and ethical guidelines. For example, if our supervisee has a case where she is working with a poor, female client and the client has been unable to get her doctor to call her back, we can teach our supervisees how to empower their clients to take action and, sometimes, have our supervisees do the advocacy for the client. We can use this as an opportunity to teach the supervisee to get the proper authorization to release information and then have our supervisee call the doctor and model to her client in the next session. We are teaching our supervisees that their work with clients and therapeutic care is influential. They have power and privilege and we are teaching the supervisee to use it to help their clients who are being marginalized to get the services they need and deserve to have. When asked what it meant for an MFT to do social justice work, one supervisee noted "I feel that I am helping clients

Table 4 Check-in questions for social justice and advocacy

How have you witnessed your supervisor being an advocate of social justice?
What has been helpful in the way your supervisor encouraged you to value social justice work?
What does it mean to you to see MFT work as social justice work?

take back the identity that has been stolen from them. I am helping them identify issues that have been holding them back from reaching their full potential." When our supervisees reach this place of understanding about social justice, we know they are coming from a place of considering power, privilege, and biases.

Our hope with advocacy is not only to assist our clients, but also to educate and challenge the many institutions that function in inequitable ways. In discussing social justice with our supervisees, they saw their work as MFTs as empowering people, giving people a voice, making a difference in the world and in the lives of their clients, engaging in the process of change in relationships where the balance of power may be unequal (Table 4).

Conclusion

As supervisors, we need to be intentional about and open to receiving honest feedback in order for social justice to be advanced and for supervision to feel safe. The four parts of the CARE model along with the check-in questions allow us to know if our intentions as supervisors align with our supervisees' experiences. Increased safety and social justice encountered in supervisory relationships will hopefully impact the safety and social justice experienced in clients' lives.

References

Adams, D. (Ed.). (1995). *Health issues for women of color: A cultural diversity perspective.* Thousand Oaks, CA: Sage.

Adichie, C. *The danger of a single story* [Video file]. Retrieved from https://www.youtube.com/watch?v=D9Ihs241zeg

Burnham, J., Alvis Palma, D., & Whitehouse, L. (2008). Learning as a context for differences and differences as a context for learning. *Journal of Family Therapy, 30*, 529–542. doi:10.1111/j.1467-6427.2008.00436.x

Crenshaw, K. (1993). Demarginalizing the interaction of race and sex: A Black feminist critique of antidiscrimination doctrine, feminist theory, and antiracist politics. In D. Wiesberg (Ed.), *Feminist legal theory: Foundations* (pp. 255–287). Stanford, CA: Stanford University Press.

Divac, A., & Heaphy, G. (2005). Space for GRRAACCES: Training for cultural competence in supervision. *Family Therapy, 27*, 0163–4445.

Greenwald, A. G., McGhee, D. E., & Schwartz, J. L. (1998). Measuring individual differences in implicit cognition: The implicit association test. *Journal of Personality and Social Psychology, 74*(6), 1464–1480.

Hook, J. N., Davis, D. E., Owen, J., Worthington, E. L., Jr., & Utsey, S. O. (2013). Cultural humility: Measuring openness to culturally diverse clients. *Journal of Counseling Psychology*. doi:10.1037/a0032595

Nadal, K. L., Griffin, K. E., Wong, Y., Hamit, S., & Rasmus, M. (2014). The impact of racial microaggressions on mental health: Counseling implications for clients of color. *Journal of Counseling and Development, 92*, 57–66. doi:10.1002/j.1556-6676.2014.00130.x

Nieto, L., & Boyer, M. (2006, March). Understanding oppression: Strategies in addressing power and privilege. *Colors NW*, 30-33.

Pendry, N. (2012). Race, racism and systemic supervision. *Journal of Family Therapy, 34*, 403–418. doi:10.1111/j.1467-6427.2011.00576.x

Stanley, D., Phelps, E., & Banaji, M. (2008). The neural basis of implicit attitudes. *Current Directions in Psychological Science, 17*(2), 164–170.

Deihl, L., & Ellis, M. V. (2009a). *The contribution of the supervisory working alliance to burnout and vigor among residential counseling paraprofessionals* (Unpublished doctoral dissertation). University at Albany, NY.

Deihl, L., & Ellis, M. V. (2009b). *The relevance of the supervisory working alliance in the supervision of residential frontline staff.* Paper presented at the Fifth international conference on clinical supervision, Buffalo, NY.

De Reus, L. A., Few, A. L., Blume, L. B. (2005). Multicultural and critical race feminisms: Theorizing families in the third wave. In: V. L. Bengtson, A. C. Acock, K. R. Allen, P. Dilworth-Anderson, & D. M. Klein. (Eds.). *Sourcebook of family theory and research* (2nd ed., pp. 447-467). Thousand Oaks, CA: Sage.

Fama, L., & Ellis, M. V. (2005). *Vicarious traumatization: A concern for doctoral level psychology trainees?* Paper presented at the 113th Annual Convention of the American Psychological Association, Washington, DC.

Hardy, K. V., & Laszloffy, T. A. (1995). The cultural genogram: Key to training culturally competent family therapists. *Journal of Marital and Family Therapy, 21*, 227–237.

Hardy, K. V., & Laszloffy, T. A. (2002). The cultural genogram: An application. In C. Storm & T. Todd (Eds.), *The reasonably complete systemic supervisor resources guide* (pp. 34–39). New York, NY: iUniverse.

Inman, A. G. (2006). Supervisor multicultural competence and its relation to supervisory process and outcome. *Journal of Marital and Family Therapy, 32*(1), 73–85.

Killian, K. D. (2001). Differences making a difference: Cross-cultural interactions in supervisory relationships. *Journal of Feminist Family Therapy, 30*, 113–129.

Ladany, N., Ellis, M. V., & Friedlander, M. L. (1999). The working alliance in clinical supervision: Relations with trainees' self-efficacy and satisfaction. *Journal of Counseling and Development, 77*, 447–455.

Zimmerman, T., Castronova, M., & ChenFeng, J. (2015). Diversity and social justice in supervision. In K. Jordan (Ed.), *Couple, marriage, and family therapy supervision* (pp. 121–168). New York, NY: Springer.

Towards Safe and Equitable Relationships: Sociocultural Attunement in Supervision

Lana Kim, Elisabeth Esmiol Wilson, Jessica ChenFeng, and Carmen Knudson-Martin

Sociocultural attunement seeks to apprehend human experience through the lenses of power and context. This relational process has been theoretically understood as the fulcrum of therapeutic change in couple's therapy (e.g., Knudson-Martin & Huenergardt, 2010, 2015), but has not yet been applied to the supervisory context. Applying sociocultural attunement to supervision represents a significant departure from supervision as an instructional, supportive process focused primarily on modalities, theories, and case conceptualization. Instead, when we center sociocultural emotion (SCE) in the supervision system, we intentionally assume a value stance that attunement to emotion as a sociocultural experience is at the heart of relationship building and is critical for the change process—for both client and the supervisee. In so doing, we honor the intersectional identities of ourselves, our supervisees, and our clients.

We are female faculty members and supervisors in COAMFTE-accredited master's programs in California, Oregon, and Washington. Lana is second-generation Korean Canadian, born and raised in Canada. Until recently, she supervised family therapy students in Georgia. Elisabeth is a European American raised in Hawaii. Jessica is second-generation Taiwanese American, born and raised in southern California. Carmen is a European American of Scandinavian heritage raised in

L. Kim, Ph.D. (✉) • C. Knudson-Martin, Ph.D.
Department of Counseling Psychology, Lewis & Clark College, Portland, OR, USA
e-mail: lkim@lclark.edu; carmen@lclark.edu

E.E. Wilson, Ph.D.
Department of Marriage and Family Therapy, Pacific Lutheran University, Tacoma, WA, USA
e-mail: esmiolev@plu.edu

J. ChenFeng, Ph.D.
Department of Educational Psychology & Counseling, California State University Northridge, Northridge, CA, USA
e-mail: jessica.chen@csun.edu

R. Allan, S.S. Poulsen (eds.), *Creating Cultural Safety in Couple and Family Therapy*, AFTA SpringerBriefs in Family Therapy,
DOI 10.1007/978-3-319-64617-6_6

North Dakota. We were initially all part of a group who developed Socio-Emotional Relationship Therapy, while working with a very diverse population in Southern California. In this chapter, we first describe three foundational premises, then discuss the sociocultural supervisory system, the supervisory skills needed to attune to sociocultural emotion (SCE), the process of attuning to supervisees' SCE, and the isomorphic process of helping supervisees attune to their clients. We illustrate with examples throughout.

What Is Attunement to Sociocultural Emotion?

Supervision grounded in attunement to SCE mirrors our approach to clinical practice and is based on three premises: (1) We begin with sociocultural attunement that seeks to go beyond awareness or understanding to experience resonance at an affective level; (2) This involves a socio-contextual theory of emotion that cannot be separated from intersecting power positions of one's social location (Wetherell, 2012); and (3) Potential for therapeutic change necessitates activating the social engagement system (Porges, 2009), a neurobiological process in which the experience of "feeling felt" (Siegel, 2001, p. 68) opens one to another and enables safety, healing, and transformation through relationship (Cozolino, 2016; van der Kolk, 2014).

Social Context of Emotion

Emotion is a link between individuals and their societal contexts. Noticing supervisees' emotions and expanding our lens to understand their context and resonate with it is an important first step in socioculturally attuned supervision and practice. Emotion arises intersubjectively in the small daily moments of our sociopolitically located worlds; it is simultaneously social and physical as social experience is created and registered in the body through an interactive sequence (Wetherell, 2012). For example, in a recent supervision session, Margie was showing her work with a white, cisgender heterosexual couple. She had been working on getting the male partner to attune to his wife. He seemed interested in doing this, but was not making much progress. Using SCE attunement as a guiding lens, the supervisor (Carmen) tried to take in Margie's sociocultural experience with the couple at a visceral level (e.g., Pandit, ChenFeng, & Kang, 2015). Carmen knew Margie was identified as a gay cisgender woman and that she was about the same age and socioeconomic status as the couple. She wondered how Margie responded emotionally in the midst of the gendered power dynamic in this relationship and what hindered her ability to "get" each partner's affective experience and respond in a clinically helpful way. Carmen also was attentive to Margie's experience as a gay person being observed by a much older and experienced cisgender heterosexual woman.

Power and Emotion

We agree with Wetherell (2012) that emotion experienced in any societal context is always connected in some way to the power dynamics inherent in the situation. In order to apprehend and emotionally resonate with Margie, Carmen tried to orient herself to Margie's power positions in this situation through questions generated out of interest regarding her experience. Softening her voice out of respect for the power imbalance between them, she began with curiosity about Margie's emotional experience while also attentive to possible power dynamics:

> Carmen: Margie, as you talk about [male client] you seem somewhat at a loss, almost as though you are defeated.
>
> Margie: Yeah. I do feel defeated. It's frustrating! I just seem stuck. All he does is smile and be agreeable, but he doesn't seem to really try to change anything.
>
> Carmen: What is it like for you trying to "get" his experience as a heterosexual man?
>
> Margie: [thoughtful pause] It's pretty familiar to me. I've seen a lot of men like him. They make me really frustrated. It's like they just write you off!
>
> Carmen: (softly) It must be hard to attune to him when you feel discounted; that male power really affects you.
>
> Margie: Ya. I don't like it. I try to stay away from it.

Margie's feelings of frustration and sense of helplessness as a therapist were connected to her one-down position in the societal gender and sexuality hierarchies. Once she was more attuned to her own experience, she was better able to attune to her client and responsively challenge the power dynamic (Sutherland, Turner, & Dienhart, 2013). When she opened herself to take in his experience, she "got" that he felt the power associated with masculinity as a need to "be a rock" and "solve the problems." His smile helped him hide his discomfort and sense of incompetence when Margie challenged the power dynamic and invited him to step down from a position of authority to attune to his wife.

Social Engagement System

According to Porges (2009), our neurological systems develop in coordination with others. When we are "held in someone else's mind and heart" (van der Kolk, 2014, p. 81), we feel calm and safe and more able to try new things that create new relationship patterns, and concurrently, are embodied in new neural pathways. In the example above, both Margie and her client were temporarily caught in a physiological state of fear inspired by their societal power positions and prior experience. The supervisor's empathic attunement to Margie's SCE enabled her to open the social engagement system in session through similar attunement to her client's emotion. Margie's ability to stay in attuned engagement with him as he first resisted and then attempted to attune to his wife was an important step toward creating an equitable and safe foundation for therapy.

Sociocultural Supervision System

We think of supervision as a triadic relational process that requires attention to the social location of all members in the system: The supervisor, trainee, and client. However, a triad only captures the most basic unit, since supervision systems often include multiple supervisees and clients. They are meaningfully shaped as supervisor, supervisees, and clients intersect across race and ethnicity, age, gender, sexual orientation, class, and the corresponding lived experiences of privilege, power, and marginalization. How each person views and engages with the therapeutic problem and change process, as well as how the supervisory process gets negotiated and experienced, further impacts the larger supervision system.

Managing Hierarchy and Negotiating Power in the System

Similar to creating the conditions for change in the therapeutic process, there is a need for supervisors and supervisees to co-create a sense of safety and trust for honest connection in the learning environment. This enables development and growth to take place. However, because of the inherent hierarchy between the supervisor and supervisees, it is incumbent upon supervisors to lead in thoughtfully acknowledging and being accountable for their power. This fosters mutuality that makes it safe for the supervisee to fully engage. The complex intersectionalities of sociopolitical power positions and social locations of the system's members present tensions that need to be uniquely negotiated. For example, in a supervisory system consisting of a White, older, upper SES, cisgender male, experienced supervisor, and a young, Mexican-American, middle SES, cisgender female, novice supervisee, an inherent power difference could be felt. The supervisor would need to pay attention to the power dynamic in a different way than the supervisee. If their roles were reversed, how power was managed would also change.

Without tuning into our supervisees' SCE and using our perceptions of their experience to guide and direct our ways of working, we may miss how power and sociocultural context frame therapy and supervision, as well as the relational aspects of learning. We may overly focus on giving explanations of therapy concepts and offering recommendations to enhance supervisee's work and overlook the way this amplifies the power difference. Learning is stifled in environments where one feels evaluated, criticized, or misunderstood, and these situations can inadvertently lead supervisees to feel defensive, silenced, and withdrawn.

At times, didactic instruction, directives, or instructional critique may be necessary to help therapists shift their practice towards greater sociocultural attunement. In instances where a supervisee may be working too heavily from a purely theoretical and distanced stance and struggling to attune to the client's SCE, the supervisor may take a more directive role and explicitly ask the therapist to consider questions designed to better understand the client's experience.

Making Mistakes and Taking Risks

We have found that intentionally seeking to attune to power, context, and SCE helps to facilitate a context of cultural humility and safety. Supervisees can therefore dialogue more openly with one another and the supervisor around instances where mistakes are made or something is missed that relates to an important aspect of a supervisee or client's intersectionality. Attuning to supervisees' SCE and taking accountability when supervisors make mistakes related to SCE encourages supervisees to take risks, accept client and supervisor feedback, and worry less about their own performance.

Case Example

During a group supervision session, Carl, a cisgender, heterosexual, White male therapist in his early 30s, married to an African American woman, asked for peer and supervisory feedback. After viewing his video, Lana, an Asian Canadian, heterosexual, cisgender female faculty supervisor in her 30s, began to offer feedback. She wondered aloud about his pacing in session, use of directives, and how he viewed the power dynamics between him, his White, mid 20s, cisgender, heterosexual, unmarried female co-therapist, and the client who was in her early 20s, cisgender, heterosexual, unmarried African American woman. Lana also asked about his theoretical assumptions regarding the client's stated feelings of sadness, and how his beliefs about the problem were shaping his approach in session.

Members of the supervision group offered their perspectives, except Shan, a cisgender, heterosexual, African American woman in her 20s who sat quietly but looked visibly concerned. Carl noticed this and asked Shan if she would share. After a pause, Shan took a risk and shared her perspective. Imagining herself as the client, she described frustration that Carl's directive approach lacked curiosity and consciousness regarding the gendered and racialized experiences in the client's day-to-day life that shaped the problem she was bringing to therapy. Shan voiced concern that if the therapy process had continued as it had, it would have been unwittingly oppressive to the client's experience.

Shan took a risk to bring race overtly into the conversation and did so from a marginalized position. Lana, while also a racially marginalized woman, held latent power because of her supervisory status and missed what Shan had understood. Lana had inadvertently relied on Shan to speak up and raise the group's critical consciousness. Realizing this, the last thing Lana wanted to do was somehow take credit for Shan's work. So, she assumed a decentered position, but held space and conveyed that she was present by "leaning in." By stepping back from trying to steer the conversation, she ensured that she did not "own" what Shan had clearly offered Carl and the group as a whole.

As the supervision group members processed their own internal SCE in relation to the dialogue Shan and Carl had shared, Lana acknowledged how not bringing in a critical perspective had created blind spots that kept her from seeing what Shan had noticed, and how she was impacted by learning to "see" through Shan's eyes. Carl responded with visible emotion as he thanked Shan for her honesty and for

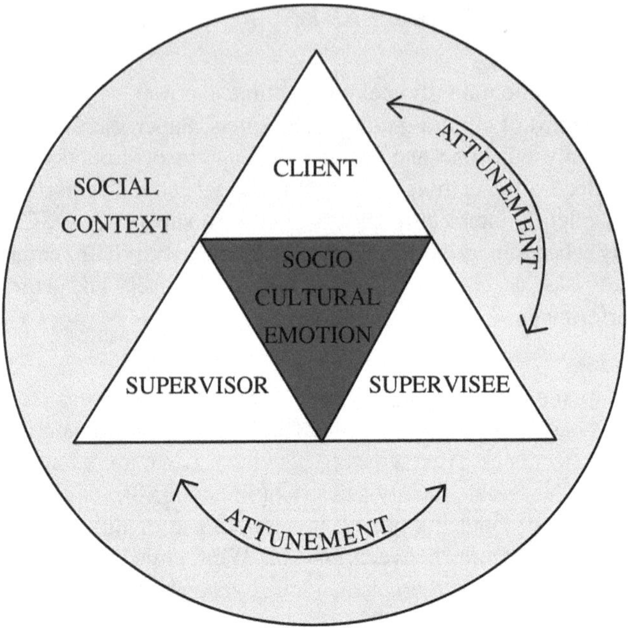

Fig. 1 Sociocultural attunement in the supervisory system

helping him become aware of his areas for growth around privilege and accountability in clinical practice. Acknowledging mistakes in SCE attunement facilitated safety and encouraged further risk-taking.

Isomorphic Processes: Supervisor to Supervisee and Supervisee to Clients

Attending to "… cultural issues and issues of power, oppression, and privilege within the supervisory relationship is an important step in helping [supervisees] to be able to do the same with their clients" (Glosoff & Durham, 2010, p. 118). In this section, we expand the application of results from a study of therapists' experience of sociocultural attunement (Pandit et al., 2015) to include supervisors in their work with supervisees (as identified by the bidirectional attunement arrows in Fig. 1). Three phases take place concurrently and are recursive: the therapist's guiding lens, sociocultural interpretation, and client and therapist resonance.

Table 1 Questions supervisors can ask self to develop a supervisory guiding lens

1. What types of experiences has the supervisee had around personal, interpersonal, and institutional power that could be present in the supervisory relationship?
2. How does the supervisee's relationship with larger systems impact constructions of self and relationships?
3. What messages about (social location identifier) has the supervisee internalized?

Therapist's Guiding Lens

Sociocultural attunement begins with a conceptual guiding lens that allows the therapist to observe and make connections with the client's SCE. This framework is not about understanding all possible discourses and contextual issues that clients from various intersecting social locations might face. Rather, it is about the link between emotion and social context, and then being curious in conversation with clients about their sociocultural experiences.

Therapeutic relationship. Supervisors may provide articles around topics of understanding social context, power and oppression, and sociocultural discourses as a way to support supervisees' development of this guiding lens. More importantly, as the supervisor models how to focus on social context in conceptualizing cases, supervisees will develop their own guiding lens. For example, when supervising a case with a heterosexual couple, the supervisor might name oppressive gender discourses such as, "women should be responsible for relationships" (ChenFeng & Galick, 2015, p. 46). These can be further discussed to explore how the supervisee might observe this discourse happening in and out of the therapy room.

Supervisory relationship. Supervisors also need to apply a sociocultural guiding lens in order to attune to SCE as discussed earlier and to bring contextual conversations into the supervisory process. When the supervisor attunes to the supervisee (as Carmen did with Margie above), there could be a discussion about what knowledge base contributed to their understanding. Supervisors can ask themselves socioculturally attuned questions to develop their guiding lens (see Table 1).

Sociocultural Interpretation

Therapeutic relationship. Application of the guiding lens enables a sociocultural interpretation of what therapists see, hear, or feel. This involves (1) internal dialogue, and (2) observable actions.

Internally, therapists listen for social discourses and link these to clients' emotions and behaviors. Therapists then bring out these internal conversations through observable actions of questioning, reflecting, validating, and naming. Therapists ask clients questions to better understand social discourses that could be impacting their experience: "Can you help me understand how the strict religious upbringing you experienced may have influenced your ideas about who you are and who you thought you ought to be?" The therapist reflects and validates an understanding of the client's sociocultural experiences: "So it sounds like now, you are feeling a lot more accepted by your church community and free to be yourself." Naming goes one step further to explicitly connect clients' emotions, experiences, and processes with the sociocultural context: "It makes sense that having a pastor and church community that accepts your sexual identity really transforms how you feel; being in this new environment where other members of your faith community are celebrating you leads you to feel loved and loveable."

Supervisory relationship. Supervisors can use this sociocultural interpretation in supervision as well. It is important to be aware of the social discourses present in supervisees' contexts and how these shape their way of engaging with their supervisor. Does the supervisee speak timidly or tentatively, or boldly and exacting, and how might this be connected to our disparate social locations as well as the power dynamics in our supervisory relationship? Is a supervisee's frustration or anger connected to feeling dismissed or unseen in our relationship? When we routinely practice these internal dialogues, we develop an ability to verbalize them with supervisees by asking questions, validating, reflecting, and naming, so they will feel attuned to and a greater sense of trust can be established in the supervisory relationship.

Client and Therapist Resonance

Therapeutic relationship. The third phase is about clients "feeling felt" (Siegel, 2001) and therapists seeing outward signs of this taking place as clients respond to their attempts. When clients resonate with the therapist's attunement, they indicate feeling felt through important paralinguistic cues. For example, clients respond by disclosing more, nodding, maintaining eye contact, and continuing with the conversation. When they do not resonate, they might disagree with the therapist, get defensive, get angry, avoid eye contact, look blank or confused, repeat themselves, or change the subject. A supervisor can support supervisees in noticing signs of client resonance by doing live supervision or watching videos of sessions and deconstructing moments where this occurs.

The second part of this phase is the therapist's resonance. Because of how humans are relationally wired and the capacity for their mirror neurons to intuit the internal experience of another (Siegel, 2001), when there is client resonance, therapist resonance follows—an emotional and physiological connection that the therapist viscerally feels towards the client. Supervisors can help supervisees attend to their own physiological experiences during sessions and teach them how to notice their visceral experience as indicators of sociocultural attunement by sharing about their own visceral experiences and curiously asking the supervisees about theirs. For example, a supervisor might say, "I felt my neck grow warm and felt a sense of sadness when the client described feeling judged as a disabled woman for losing her baby. I imagine her experience of discrimination affects her grief. I noticed you sort of held your breath too. What was happening for you? How do you understand who she is in the world around her, and how does this affect the way you get her story and engage with her?"

Supervisory relationship. As supervisors seek to understand supervisees' sociocultural worlds, we need to attend to whether our understanding actually aligns with the supervisees' experience. When supervisees feel felt, they will feel safer to ask questions and engage as though they have something to contribute. Supervisors will also feel more connected, creating positive energy that enhances trust. Supervisees can subsequently learn how to attune to their clients' needs by the modeling we do in attuning to their needs (Friedlander, 2012).

Necessary Supervisory Skills

Relational power dynamics and the larger cultural context intimately shape experiences in supervision and therapy. The sociocultural emotions of each member in these systems are more than helpful information, but rather a vital path towards growth and change. Change happens through the experience of feeling another person attuned to one's own SCE. Yet attuning to supervisees across multiple differences in intersecting identities requires a complex set of supervisory skills. Elisabeth, a middle class, White, cisgender female, faculty supervisor in her 30s was working with Mia, a working class, Latina, cisgendered female, graduate student in her early 20s. As Elisabeth tried to attune to Mia's SCE, her hope was that Mia might begin to experience a deeper understanding of the impact of her own context on her emotional experiences. Elisabeth also hoped Mia might be able to more intentionally and accurately attune to her clients' SCE. Yet Elisabeth would need to regularly hone and practice the following seven specific self-of-the-supervisor skills in order to remain sensitively attuned to Mia, especially given the differences in their context and social location.

1. *Utilizing a sociocultural attunement framework.* Before attuning to Mia, Elisabeth needs to understand the importance of SCE. Specifically, she needs to see the necessity of attuning to supervisees' and clients' unique felt experiences of power differentials and cultural context. She must also be able to understand and articulate the necessity of attunement to SCE in the therapeutic change process.
2. *Socially locate one's self.* Elisabeth also needs to identify her own social location, for example, "I identify as a middle class White, heterosexual, cisgender female, progressive Christian, and remarried mother and stepmother." Part of socially locating herself will include naming her unearned privilege and purposely inviting and co-creating a more mutual power dynamic in supervision. Elisabeth needs to thoughtfully socially locate herself with supervisees, such as Mia, in order to openly discuss how their different intersecting identities could potentially both benefit and limit their supervisory relationship (Watts-Jones, 2010). For supervisors with less unearned privilege, socially locating oneself

may include naming specific areas of marginalization, discrimination, and oppression. As supervisors socially locate themselves, they model how identities with intersecting unearned privilege and marginalization/oppression can be authentically and honorably engaged within relationship.

3. *Validate one's own SCE.* After socially locating herself, Elisabeth must be able to name and validate her own experiences of SCE. For Elisabeth, this includes exploring the emotional impact of owning her White privilege, her internalized racism, as well as privilege associated with her class, profession, and education level. She will need to be able to move beyond White guilt and fragility to taking responsibility and acknowledging her own unearned privilege. She will also need to explore how gendered power and experiences of sexism impact her sociocultural emotions, both professionally and personally. For a supervisor with more marginalized experiences, this process may include validating emotions such as fear or anger, resisting and redefining stereotypes, and moving towards genuine self-expression (Nieto & Boyer, 2010).
4. *Tolerate discomfort.* Another skill Elisabeth needs before attuning to Mia's SCE is the ability to handle difficult emotions within herself and in others. Supervisors need to self-regulate their own emotions when working with issues of power, privilege, and marginalization and the corresponding sociocultural emotions (Garcia, Kosutic, & McDowell, 2015). Clinicians tend to move away from the emotional discomfort of such work due to fear of being disrespectful (Vargas & Wilson, 2011). Rather than shutting down her own and others' emotions, Elisabeth must learn to regulate her own discomfort in order to tolerate Mia's potentially difficult, painful, and angry sociocultural emotions. Elisabeth might do this through personal mindfulness and breathing activities, accountability groups with other supervisors, holding onto curiosity, directly inviting Mia to share about her contextual differences, and asking Mia to provide Elisabeth with regular feedback on the supervisory relationship and experience.
5. *Pursue SCE.* Once Elisabeth can tolerate difficult sociocultural emotions, the next skill involves pursuing such emotion. The path to pursuing such uncomfortable emotions requires seeing SCE as a pathway to healing. Elisabeth must learn to move towards, draw out, and heighten her own and Mia's SCE as a path to professional growth and development. This might involve asking questions and also making the direct link between felt experiences and the larger societal and cultural context. For example, Elisabeth might notice that Mia becomes quieter when working with Max, an older, White, cisgender male client. As they talk about Mia's clinical work, Elisabeth might wonder about Mia's experience of Max as an older White man. Elisabeth may further wonder with Mia about her experiences in the larger society with older White adults, for example, having to work harder to prove herself, and the impact on Mia of working with Elisabeth, an older White female supervisor, and the impact on Mia's experience as Max's therapist.
6. *Demonstrate supervisory leadership.* Supervisory leadership can look very different based on our own social location and our model of supervision. For Elisabeth, taking a one-down position with Mia was essential to building the

safety and shared power necessary for Mia to explore her SCE linked to her struggles with Max. For a more marginalized supervisor, navigating a collaborative relationship while maintaining the power of a didactic supervisory role may be more nuanced. How we negotiate power is directly linked to the intersecting identities of both the supervisor and supervisee. The danger is losing the didactic role of providing instructional critique. Supervisors need to instruct, and while different models of supervision instruct very differently, attuning to SCE provides a framework from which a supervisor can offer more accurate, contextualized, supervisee-informed feedback. Attuning involves a real connection that influences and changes each person, while actively demonstrating supervisory leadership.

7. *Practice psychological resonance.* Finally, Elisabeth needs to hone through regular practice the skill of attuning or providing that psychological resonance of giving Mia the experience of feeling felt. Elisabeth needs to move beyond empathy to non-verbally mirroring what Mia is feeling and experiencing, moment by moment. The neurological research on mirror neurons indicates that as Elisabeth achieves this, Mia and Elisabeth will actually be in a state of shared resonance from which potentially healing experiences will emerge (Cozolino, 2016). Such healing may include a corrective experience for Mia with a White authority figure intentionally and collaboratively sharing power in their relationship. Healing may also include Mia experiencing validation for and recognition of the reality of the oppression, trauma, and microaggressions she and her community experience. Finally, healing may include Mia experiencing her supervisor as someone who is open to learning from and growing with Mia in their shared supervisory relationship.

Process of Attuning to Supervisee's Sociocultural Emotion

A reflexive supervision process where the supervisor is willing to offer their own work and internal process and be emotionally accessible leads to emotional closeness and bonding in the supervisory relationship (Mangione, Mears, Vincent, & Hawes, 2011). We believe that in addition to offering our own experiences to supervisees, we must be curious about and attentive to supervisees' emotional experiences. Not doing so allows us to maintain our supervisory power and distance and we can miss out on significant areas of growth.

Case Example

Anna was a Chinese American cisgender woman in her 20s attending supervision with Jessica, a Taiwanese American cisgender woman in her 30s. Below we describe how Jessica addressed social context and SCE with Anna. In so doing, they were mutually empowered and shared in developing critical consciousness.

Socially locating. Jessica was supervising Anna in a practicum setting, while Anna was an MFT student. Anna was respectful and deferential to her professors and supervisors and expected to engage with Jessica as her elder. Jessica knew that it was her responsibility as the supervisor to initiate conversations about social location (Hird, Cavalieri, Dulko, Felice, & Ho, 2001) so they could establish a collaborative working relationship and so Jessica could give her permission to interact in new ways than what she might have assumed was appropriate.

From the beginning, Jessica shared about her social location, particularly the areas that would be relevant to their relationship (race/ethnicity, age, gender, SES). Jessica's sharing about her background as a Taiwanese American woman and her experiences in the field gave Anna permission to talk about her racial/ethnic identity in supervision. In being curious about why Anna entered the MFT field, Jessica asked questions around Anna's social context and how these were influences in her decision.

Connecting emotional experience to social context. Early on, it was clear that Anna felt a general discomfort around clinical work; this presented as her feeling incompetent and discouraged about her skills. Rather than accepting the perspective that Anna was an incompetent clinician and subsequently focusing on building her skills, Jessica wanted to understand what this discouragement was about. She learned that Anna was the only Asian American in her class cohort and that her classmates were "so natural" at doing therapy and this made her feel like she was the only one wrestling with whether or not she was good enough. They had a professor who encouraged emotion-focused work and she saw her classmates being able to talk openly and freely about emotions, whereas she felt tongue-tied. Jessica did not want to assume that what she knew about Asian American values (i.e., having emotional self-control) was necessarily true for Anna. Yet, when they talked about it, Anna shared that indeed this was a significant part of her context and that it was rude and disrespectful to directly ask someone about their feelings.

Mutual empowerment. As this part of her SCE was validated and re-interpreted as not being a fault or flaw, Anna was freed to see herself as having much to contribute. She did not have to try so hard to fit into field expectations and discourses shaped by dominant Western culture. Her Chinese American identity was an asset and it was important for Jessica as her supervisor to receive this and to consider how to walk alongside her towards integrating her sociocultural system with clinical work. As an Asian American female supervisor, Jessica felt affirmed and empowered in choosing to talk openly about social location, especially through witnessing Anna's transformation.

Conclusion

The supervisory relationship has the capacity to impact multiple systemic levels. When supervisors attune and attend to supervisees' SCE reality, they are building a strong working alliance with supervisees, raising critical consciousness together, being mutually empowered, and modeling how attunement can be done with clients. The supervisor is not doing this *for* the supervisee, but rather we are suggesting that the supervisory relationship is a place where cultural equity (Rigazio-DiGilio, 2014) is lived out. Both supervisor and supervisee are connecting with themselves, each other, and their disparate/shared social contexts, and in so doing, contributing to a dynamic where influence is being given and received on all levels. As supervisors, we position ourselves in a way where seeking to attune to supervisee's sociocultural emotion is as much about our self-awareness and critical consciousness as it is about doing this with supervisees.

References

ChenFeng, J. L., & Galick, A. (2015). How gender discourses hijack couple therapy—and how to avoid it. In C. Knudson-Martin, M. A. Wells, & S. K. Samman (Eds.), *Socio-emotional relationship therapy: Bridging emotion, societal discourse, and couple interaction* (pp. 41–52). New York, NY: Springer.

Cozolino, L. (2016). *Why therapy works: Using our minds to change our brains*. New York, NY: Norton.

Friedlander, M. L. (2012). Therapist responsiveness: Mirrored in supervisor responsiveness. *The Clinical Supervisor, 31*(1), 103–119. doi:10.1080/07325223.2012.675199

Garcia, M., Košutic, I., & McDowell, T. (2015). Peace on earth/war at home: The role of emotion regulation in social justice work. *Journal of Feminist Family Therapy, 27*, 1–20. doi:10.1080/08952830802683673

Glosoff, H. L., & Durham, J. C. (2010). Using supervision to prepare social justice counseling advocates. *Counselor Education and Supervision, 50*(2), 116–129. doi:10.1002/j.1556-6978.2010.tb00113.x

Hird, J. S., Cavalieri, C. E., Dulko, J. P., Felice, A. A., & Ho, T. A. (2001). Visions and realities: Supervisee perspectives of multicultural supervision. *Journal of Multicultural Counseling and Development, 29*(2), 114–130. doi:10.1002/j.2161-1912.2001.tb00509.x

Knudson-Martin, C., & Huenergardt, D. (2010). A socio-emotional approach to couple therapy: Linking social context and couple interaction. *Family Process, 49*, 369–368. doi:10.1111/j.1545-5300.2010.01328.x

Knudson-Martin, C., & Huenergardt, D. (2015). Bridging emotion, societal discourse, and couple interaction in clinical practice. In C. Knudson-Martin, M. A. Wells, & S. K. Samman (Eds.), *Socio-emotional relationship therapy: Bridging emotion, societal context, and couple interaction* (pp. 1–13). New York, NY: Springer.

Mangione, L., Mears, G., Vincent, W., & Hawes, S. (2011). The supervisory relationship when women supervise women: An exploratory study of power, reflexivity, collaboration, and authenticity. *The Clinical Supervisor, 30*(2), 141–171. doi:10.1080/07325223.2011.604272

Nieto, L., & Boyer, M. (2010). Beyond inclusion, beyond empowerment: *A developmental strategy to liberate everyone*. Lacey, WA: Cuetzpalin.

Pandit, M., ChenFeng, J. L., & Kang, Y. J. (2015). SERT therapists experience of practicing sociocultural attunement. In C. Knudson-Martin, M. A. Wells, & S. K. Samman (Eds.), *Socio-emotional relationship therapy: Bridging emotion, societal context, and couple interaction* (pp. 67–78). New York, NY: Springer.

Porges, S. W. (2009). Reciprocal influences between the body and the brain in the perception and expression of affect. In D. Fosha, D. S. Siegel, & M. F. Solomon (Eds.), *The healing power of emotion: Affective neuroscience, development & clinical practice* (pp. 27–54). New York, NY: W.W Norton.

Rigazio-DiGilio, S. A. (2014). Supervising couple and family therapy practitioners. In C. Watkins & E. Milne (Eds.), *International handbook of clinical supervision* (pp. 622–647). London, UK: Wiley-Blackwell.

Siegel, D. J. (2001). *The developing mind: How relationships and the brain intersect to shape who we are*. New York, NY: Guilford Press.

Sutherland, O., Turner, J., & Dienhart, A. (2013). Responsive persistence part I: Therapist influence in postmodern practice. *Journal of Marital and Family Therapy, 39*, 470–487. doi:10.1111/j.1752-0606.2012.00333.x

Van der Kolk, B. (2014). *The body keeps the score: Brain, mind, and body in the healing of trauma*. New York, NY: Penguin Books.

Vargas, H. L., & Wilson, C. M. (2011). Managing worldview influences: Self-awareness and self-supervision in a cross-cultural therapeutic relationship. *Journal of Family Psychotherapy, 22*, 97–113. doi:10.1080/08975353.2011.577684

Watts-Jones, T. D. (2010). Location of self: Opening the door to dialogue on intersectionality in the therapy process. *Family Process, 49*(3), 405–420. doi:10.1111/j.1545-5300.2010.01330.x

Wetherell, M. (2012). *Affect and emotion: A new social science understanding*. London, UK: Sage.

Comprehensive Multicultural Curriculum: Self-Awareness as Process

Ali Michael and Eleonora Bartoli

Clinical and counseling training has traditionally consisted of one multicultural (MC) course aimed at providing students with the minimal MC competence required for entering the profession. Multiculturalists and educators have questioned the effectiveness of this "one course" model and have urged programs either to offer multiple MC courses or to infuse MC training throughout the curriculum (e.g., David-Russell, 2003; Rogers & O'Bryon, 2014). Neither of these options is easy to implement. The "multiple courses" model is onerous given the number of professional standards that must be covered within a limited number of credits (especially within master's degree programs); the "infusion" model requires coordination as well as MC expertise among *all* faculty. These were the challenges faced by the administrators and faculty of our counselor education program when we decided to make social justice and multicultural principles core values in both our mission and objectives. The road to "multiculturalize" the program was not a linear one; however, a decade later, a new comprehensive MC counseling training is fully integrated within our program.

Our counselor education program offers a master's degree in counseling, leading students to obtain licensure as a professional counselor. The program is guided by two core orientations: evidence-based practices and multicultural counseling. The program is situated at the outskirts of a major metropolitan area in the Northeast; it attracts mostly local students, many of whom are first-generation college or graduate students, the majority of whom are White, and almost all of whom work while

A. Michael, Ph.D. (✉)
Center for the Study of Race and Equity in Education, Graduate School of Education, University of Pennsylvania, 3700 Walnut Street, Fourth Floor, Philadelphia, PA 19104, USA
e-mail: ali.s.michael@gmail.com

E. Bartoli, Ph.D.
Graduate Counseling Program, Psychology Department, Arcadia University, Glenside, PA 19038, USA

R. Allan, S.S. Poulsen (eds.), *Creating Cultural Safety in Couple and Family Therapy*, AFTA SpringerBriefs in Family Therapy,
DOI 10.1007/978-3-319-64617-6_7

attending the program (students have varied socioeconomic backgrounds). Despite the relative homogeneity of the program, the program is attended by a minority of international students, students of color, students with disabilities, nontraditional students, and LGBT students.

MC training is often described as encompassing three components: knowledge, skills, and self-awareness (Sue & Sue, 2013). The "combined" model involves crafting distinct knowledge, skills, and self-awareness curricula that could be consistently delivered across courses and faculty (Bartoli et al., 2014). While MC skills and knowledge are relatively easy to identify and quantify, MC self-awareness is much more difficult to foster and ensure (i.e., you can bring a horse to water, but you cannot make them drink!). In this paper, we share a creative solution to the above challenges that combines the one course model with the infusion model. First we will provide an overview of the overall structure of the combined model; then, we will offer a detailed description of the most impactful, but difficult to deliver, aspect of the program, i.e., the MC self-awareness Labs. These Labs challenged us as educators to move away from simply conveying content, towards enabling a transformative *process* to take place.[1]

Structure of Combined Model

The first step was to create distinct (albeit somewhat overlapping) knowledge, skills, and self-awareness curricula, based on both the program's objectives and the current MC literature. The second step was to infuse these curricula into specific *core* courses, to ensure that all students would complete the entire MC training regardless of concentration or electives chosen. The faculty teaching any one of these core courses would then be responsible for delivering the relevant section of the curriculum. The new curriculum was originally developed by two core faculty (the second author, who is a White, cisgender, bisexual, spiritual, and able-bodied woman, and an African American faculty member, who is identified as a cisgender lesbian woman, who is able-bodied and spiritual). Both faculty members have conducted research on religion, race, and multiculturalism in psychology. Also, on the team was an adjunct faculty member (an African American, cisgender, heterosexual, and able-bodied woman)—all clinicians with expertise in multicultural counseling. That team then invited a colleague (the first author) with expertise in anti-racist education to further develop the self-awareness Labs. The first author is a White, heterosexual, Jewish, middle class, able-bodied, and cisgender woman, whose published work focuses on making research on race and education more accessible to teachers. The Labs utilized her experience of helping people from mainstream groups understand privilege and oppression with regard to race and other social identities.

[1] The second author is the director of the program in question and the first author was hired to develop and deliver the multicultural self-awareness labs based on the goals laid out by a committee from the department.

The curriculum is currently integrated into six core courses: an introductory psychopathology course (prerequisite for all other courses), two sequential counseling skill courses, a multicultural counseling course, and two sequential internship courses. The curriculum is also delivered via two sets of Labs (MC self-awareness Labs, and MC knowledge Labs); each Lab consists of two sections of 9 h of training over three sessions, for a total of 36 h over 12 sessions (almost the equivalent of an additional course). The two MC self-awareness Labs are attached[2] to the introductory psychopathology course and the first counseling skill course; the two MC knowledge Labs are attached to the internship courses. Structurally, the knowledge curriculum is envisioned to be delivered primarily in the multicultural counseling course as well as the two MC knowledge Labs. The skills curriculum is delivered primarily in the introductory psychopathology course and in the two counseling skills courses. The self-awareness curriculum is delivered primarily in the multicultural counseling course as well as the two MC self-awareness Labs.

In terms of content, the MC knowledge curriculum covers concepts related to MC assessment and diagnosis, as well as the history and primary concerns of given populations. The MC self-awareness curriculum invites students to understand and explore their mainstream (or privileged) and marginalized (or oppressed) sociopolitical identities; track their biases and multicultural countertransference; learn how to remain engaged in culturally charged dialogues; and identify their need for additional training, allies, and accountability for ongoing self-work. The MC skills curriculum trains students to assess and diagnose considering cultural variables; build and maintain a strong therapeutic alliance with individuals across differences in social identities; raise questions of a MC nature while investigating the familial, communal, and cultural influences impacting clients' symptomatology; infuse multicultural considerations into case conceptualization; and deliver MC interventions, or know when to culturally tailor traditional interventions.

The task in developing the knowledge and skills curricula was to perform a thorough review of the literature and cohesively infuse specific content and skills practice across courses taught by different faculty (for a more detailed description of the knowledge and skills curricula, as well as their implications for faculty training, see Bartoli et al., 2014). The challenge, in each case, was essentially logistical. The challenge posed by the self-awareness curriculum was quite different, as self-awareness is not as easily "quantifiable." When it came to crafting the self-awareness curriculum, our question was not simply *what* to teach, but *how* to enable a transformative process to take place within a relatively short time. The remainder of the paper will describe in more detail not simply the content of the MC self-awareness Labs, but also, and perhaps more importantly, the pedagogical strategies used to deliver these Labs. In MC training, we think of self-awareness as the cornerstone of the MC curriculum, as students' ability to appropriately use their MC knowledge

[2] The labs are attached to the courses institutionally just as chemistry labs are attached to chemistry courses, with the same cost to students (no additional cost), resources committed to the department by the institution, and requirement of completion for advancement in the program.

and skills in fact *relies* on their self-awareness. Without the latter, both MC knowledge and skills are devoid of power.

MC Self-Awareness Labs: Focus on Process

Through the MC self-awareness Labs (hereafter referred to as "the Labs"), we wanted to create a space for students to become intimately familiar with the actual chemistry of diversity, with how the different elements react when mixed together. Unlike a chemistry lab, the basic elements under inquiry are not hydrogen and oxygen, but rather the widely variable intersectional identities and experiences that our students bring to our program. Therefore, we were challenged to create a space in which students could share honestly about how their identities shape their lives, their lenses on the world, their impact on one another, and their work as counselors.

Fundamentally, the Labs were designed to help students understand themselves as individuals within the context of a larger society in which oppression and privilege play a part in their relationships with clients and colleagues. In other words, we wanted our students to understand, not only that they have a race, a gender identity and a sex, a sexual orientation, physical and mental abilities and disabilities, a class background, and a relationship to religion (whether they practice or not), but that all of these aspects of their identity contribute to the social power they wield in the world. Our students are predominantly—but not entirely—White, middle class, heterosexual, cisgender, raised Christian, physically able, young, and female, with a range of experiences with mental health. Many of them experience some marginalization as a result of their social identities, and almost all of them have at least one mainstream identity. The Labs were structured around the idea that a key rule of multiculturalism is to know one's own culture (e.g., Williams, Hayes, & Fauth, 2008); understanding others requires understanding oneself *in context,* and *as a part of the same context* as others. Because of this, students must first take time to consider how their own identities impact *them* (e.g., their lenses, their communications styles, their judgments, and their relationships with people who are similar or different from themselves). Without this self-knowledge, students could have tremendous knowledge about diverse social groups, but if they implicitly view Whiteness, middle classness, heterosexuality, cis identity, and Christianity as the norm, rather than part of the diversity of human experience, then they risk unconsciously viewing everybody who does not fit into those groups as incomplete, or worse, as deviations from the norm (Bartoli et al., 2015). The goal here is not to essentialize any one of these identities, but to help students recognize the particular ways these identities come together in them and impact how they relate to others.

We wanted to create a setting that could call attention to students' identities and then invite the students *themselves* to make meaning of them. The latter involves the use of processes designed to increase self-awareness so that students would not simply understand the concept of "identity" intellectually, but would *feel* it from the inside out. As each student shares what they are learning about themselves, they begin to understand concepts of social identity in a way that is intimately personalized, contextualized, and intersectional. Without this self-awareness, both MC knowledge and skills are devoid of power, as both must be applicable and relevant to micro-interactions.

Process permeates every aspect of the Labs, from the curriculum to the syllabus, to the organization of time in the class, and to the way grading is conducted. All students enrolled in the courses that come with a Lab are expected to enroll in the Lab. Our courses run with a minimum of 10 students and a maximum of 18 students. On occasion, students have to take the Lab portion of the class during a different semester, so the size of the Lab varies from semester to semester, but it remains fairly stable around 15 students. All Labs are facilitated by one faculty member (the first author), who is the only faculty running the Labs.

The next several sections of the paper will describe each of the six sessions of the Labs (three sessions for each semester): first its content and then the process used to make the content come alive for each student. In between the content and the process sections, we share quotes from students' final papers, in which they reflect on their learning in the Labs. As mentioned above, each Lab is attached to a required course; students are required to pass all of the Labs in order to graduate, and they must attend every Lab session in order to pass each Lab. The Labs are graded on a pass/fail basis. While we want to make it clear to students that the Labs are critically important to their training as counselors, we do not want to risk students pretending to know something in order to get a good grade. In other words, we wanted to create a space that students take seriously *and* in which they can engage in honest, introspective, exploratory self-awareness which makes the process itself, rather than the grade, the ultimate outcome of the Lab. All Labs are facilitated by the first author, who is an adjunct faculty member.

MC Self-Awareness Labs: Curriculum

Session 1: Social Construction of Identities and Styles of Communication (Theme: Gender)

Content: After orienting students to the purpose and structure of the Lab, the instructor (the first author) introduces herself both professionally and personally; students then introduce themselves by taking 1 min each to share anything about themselves with the other students. A review of the syllabus includes a discussion of the "The Four Agreements for Courageous Conversations" (Singleton and Linton, 2015) and of how students might maximize and minimize their learning and engagement in the class. The central activity of this first session focuses on the social construction of gender in the students' lives. The session then closes with a brief experiential activity designed to help students become mindful of, and therefore familiar with, the terrain of their "discomfort zones."

> Our discussion in lab about gender was very productive for me. I think it helped me feel more secure about being very gender conforming and also a strong and independent woman at the same time. I had been thinking about how those two parts of my identity could coexist before we discussed it in lab, but after lab I felt better about those two things not being mutually exclusive.[3]

Process: The first module is designed not only to give a clear structure to the labs—identifying the purpose, sharing the syllabus, and giving space for extensive introductions—but also to ensure that everyone has a voice, challenging students to consider their own contributions to building a strong learning community. The aim is to build a strong "container" within the group, which will support the group to do the hard work we are asking of them. The instructor makes herself vulnerable, sharing parts of her journey that might help students connect to her as an individual and a person still in process, with her own biases and learning curve (rather than just as an authority figure or a professional); it shows the students that she's still in a growth process herself, that we are all always learning. Further, by sharing that she grew up in a community where she knew no people of color and no out gay people, she models that wherever students are starting their journey, they can grow from that place.

The social construction of gender exercise is designed to show students the ways in which they were given messages about how to fit inside the box of their gender and the ways they in fact do not fit into their assigned box. In the process of sharing, we begin to see what it means to be "a girl" and what it means to be "a boy" in US society (e.g., "This is what it means that gender is "socially constructed." It's not about genitalia or bodies, it's about how each of us was taught a "right" way to be a "boy" or a "girl.").We discuss how most of us were socialized to be one or the other, and how very few of us were taught about gender identities outside the binary; in that context, we talk about "cisgender privilege" and trans and gender nonconforming identity.

We focus on the "discomfort zone" at the end of the session to reinforce the idea that the best learning happens when we are a little uncomfortable, and that different people are uncomfortable with different things. In fact, the goal of the Labs is to spend time in the discomfort zone and learn from such moments, rather than responding to discomfort with "fight" or "flight." In other words, if students are to learn something new about themselves, they must learn not to shut down, but rather remain open, in moments of discomfort. The homework at the end of Session 1 requires students to write about their communication styles, particularly the styles they use when they are angry or sad.

[3]The student quotes used in this chapter come directly from their final papers. All students have given their permission for the quotes to be shared anonymously.

Session 2: Examining the Culture of Privileged Groups (Theme: Religion)

Content: We start each lab session with an icebreaker that helps the group continue to get to know each other. Then students share their writing on personal communication styles in small groups, followed by an extensive debrief that invites them to consider whether their communication styles are related to their gender socialization. Next, we use an experiential activity to introduce a concrete theoretical framework for understanding mainstream group identities and marginalized group identities; the goal is for each student to understand and become more conscious about their mainstream identities (whether they are White, able-bodied, middle class, heterosexual, cisgendered, Christian, etc.), as most people tend to be inherently less conscious of their mainstream identities and of the impact of those identities on their own and others' lives. We then move to the second theme of the Lab (after gender): Religion. Students anonymously[4] share (1) how they practice (or do not practice) religion currently; (2) how they practiced (or did not practice) religion growing up; and (3) how they feel about religion. Towards the end of the session, students briefly journal about how the theory of mainstreams/margins will impact their work as counselors. To close, each person shares one sentence about their experience of the session.

> Another area of growth that I have encountered is a better tolerance for people who are not at the same juncture of their journey as I am. From the get-go, I admittedly found myself judging those who were not as aware of their privilege for instance. But, as we progressed with the lab, I was able to empathize with those people, because I too had been in their position not long before this.

Process: This second session's impact relies on the strong "container" built in the first session, which allows for the group members to genuinely connect and share. The students begin to see how the activities are structured to evoke self-reflection and open discussion not only of their identities, but also of how their identities shape their styles of interaction and presentation. Even though the content of this particular session focuses on religion, the work on communication style necessarily ties back to the students' realizations in the previous class on gender. The process work follows up on students' assignments and asks them to see their communication styles through the lens of their evolving understanding of their social identities, thus including the analysis of gender that they acquired the week before. Many students have not previously considered how their gender socialization impacts the

[4] Each student receives four scraps of paper and they are invited to write on one paper the religion they grew up with (or didn't) and the religion they practice now (or don't). On the remaining three sheets, they are invited to write three different feelings—and some explanation of those feelings—that they have about religion. These papers are then put into a basket, and mixed up. Each student draws and reads four papers aloud, and in doing so, we have the basis for a beginning conversation on our feelings and experiences with religion, based on the anonymous sharing of our own experiences.

ways they exhibit (or do not exhibit) emotions; yet those patterns emerge, and are named, during the class discussions.

Some students might also begin making connections about communication styles and their religious cultural backgrounds. To do so, the instructor "tracks" connections for students; "tracking"[5] is the practice of noticing without judgment; it is a way of calling attention to connections or group dynamics so that group members notice them and they themselves begin making sense of them. When the instructor hears a male student, who the previous week reported that he was socialized not to cry, describe his communication style as dominated by anger, she might ask whether he sees a relationship between his gender socialization and his communication style. Or when a student who had mentioned in the first class that she wanted to maximize her learning by speaking up when she did not understand or did not agree because that was typically challenging for her, the instructor may remind her of that when she talks about a communication style that is heavily shaped by trying to be invisible—and whether that, in turn, could be shaped by her religious, gender, race, or class socialization. The key here is not to link student cultural styles to stereotypes of their identities, but to the narratives that they themselves share about how their different identities manifest in their own lives. In this way, students begin to recognize the impact of their socialization.

Gender socialization is usually a good place to start because it is often felt by students to be a relatively innocuous topic. By discussing gender socialization, students start to become comfortable with the idea that their behavior, expectations, and sense of belonging or entitlement may have been influenced, in part, by parts of their social identities and by how the world responds to these identities. This is valuable as the class moves towards seeing how racial socialization and class positioning do this just as much as gender. The mainstream/margin theory challenges all students to be conscious of mainstream privilege, rather than focusing exclusively on White students to acknowledge racial privilege. This approach minimizes defensiveness on the part of White students, while expanding the consciousness of privilege on the part of all the students. In this process, the instructor shares a quote from diversity educator Rev. Dr. Jamie Washington: "We tend to live in the pain of our marginalized identities, but we tend to act out of the arrogance of our mainstream identities." The assignments for the third session are to (i) write a reflection on how it feels to have—and become aware of—one's mainstream or "privileged" identities; and (ii) take Harvard's Implicit Attitudes Test (IAT; Project Implicit, n.d.).

[5] The concept of "tracking" has been passed down to the first author through facilitation mentors such as Sarah Halley and Frederick Bryant. To the best of our knowledge, it comes from a well-known activist and facilitator named Elsie Y. Cross, founder and director of Elsie Cross and Associates.

Session 3: Examining Unconscious Bias (Theme: Race)

Content: This is the third and final session in the first Lab. We intentionally placed a discussion of unconscious bias and race after students have built their capacity to see and talk about parts of themselves that are less challenging to notice and share. In this class, students read parts of their writing on mainstream identities; then the class debriefs the sharing. The instructor reminds students that privilege is not a "blessing" or the equivalent of being "lucky;" it is the consequence of a society that has socially constructed different identities in ways that systematically advantage people with a privileged or "mainstream" identity and systematically disadvantage people with an oppressed or "marginalized" identity. It is important for students to understand that people who are oppressed or "marginalized" do not usually want to change who they are; they just want who they are to be more accepted, to need less explanation, to not be "illegal." In this context, the instructor invites students to begin noticing and recording the judgments they have made of one another, encouraging them to recognize that our judgments tell us more about ourselves than they do about others ("judgment awareness activity").

Then the class discusses the results of the IAT in small groups. The instructor shares bias reduction techniques, including loading counter-stereotypical images of groups one has bias towards onto one's phone or desktop screen; repeatedly retesting oneself using the IAT to increase consciousness of unconscious bias; or consciously subtracting value judgments (e.g., about safety, intelligence, or foreignness) when encountering a person from a heavily stereotyped group (Ross, 2014). As a group, the class talks about the impact of bias on their lives, and how it differentially impacts them depending on their race, or how they appear to others. The class closes this third session (which, again, also marks the end of the first set of self-awareness Labs) by giving each student time to say good bye and share a final statement with the class.

Lab has helped a lot because instead of running away from biases because I shouldn't have them, it has taught me to accept them and then see how these biases impact my life. Fully understanding my biases is not something that can happen in a year alone. It is going to take me a long time and make a lot of mistakes before I can get to where I want to be. It is easy to pull away from the biases when they make me feel uncomfortable, but that will not help me as a counselor.

I feel like I still view my privilege as a White person as something to be ashamed of. As if I needed to atone for the sins of the White people in our country who came before me. Through this lab I've learned that this is not the case at all. However, my mind still diverts back to this way of thinking at times when I do not have the safety net of lab and my classmates behind me.

Process: This is the class where students process their reflections on "mainstream" or privileged identities. Some semesters there is no time for the "judgment awareness activity," and that is not a problem. The goal of all activities is to stimulate deep, engaged, self-reflective conversation; if that is happening, there is no need to rush to the next activity.

The "implicit bias" conversation should be prioritized over the "judgment awareness activity" because it is an essential part of the discussion of race, usually a stirring topic for students. Sometimes, the conversation about mainstreams and margins leads directly to race, depending on how many White people choose to write about their Whiteness as a mainstream identity. Regardless, students process how it felt to take the test as well as how to understand the results. The instructor shares how she grappled with her score, acknowledging that she may never be able to achieve a score that shows she is "unbiased," and how frustrating that is for her. Students always challenge the test and wonder how a two-second difference of reaction time could possibly matter in the scope of a long-term relationship. In response, the instructor encourages students to share with one another: "Maybe it didn't impact you, but it might have impacted others. Let's hear from people who feel like there have been moments in your life when two-seconds might have made a big difference for you." After that, they are invited to consider other ways implicit bias may matter in the blink of 2 seconds, particularly in the context of the counseling profession.

This third session closes by giving students a chance to say good bye or share something they have learned. This is another critical step in building the "container" for the work, a container that outlives the labs as it supports the cohort's capacity to have challenging conversations about identity in the rest of their classes as well. This process re-affirms that the Labs are not like other classes, where most of the content is predetermined; in the Labs there is space for students to influence the content of the discussions, build community, and learn about themselves by connecting mindfully with one another. This is also a critical time for them to recognize the ways in which they have grown as individuals in just a few weeks.

Session 4: Recognizing our Triggers/Self-Acceptance (Theme: Ability)

Content: There is usually a significant time lapse (a few months) between the first and second (MC self-awareness) Labs, and even though most students take the second Lab with the same group as the first Lab, not all students' schedules allow for that to happen. However, all students attend the first three sessions, and by the time they get to the second part of the Labs, they have all built a relationship with the instructor (who remains the same for both Labs). This usually means that there is a level of trust that carries over from the prior three sessions, regardless of class composition, and that students have a sense of how safe the Lab space feels for them to talk about sometimes uncomfortable topics.

The instructor begins the session by having students share one thing they do not usually share with colleagues, and then one thing they connect to about another person in the Lab (on the basis of something they have learned about that person at another point in the graduate program). After a review of the syllabus, the session delves into the topic of dis/ability. After watching and discussing a short video of Stephen Hawking, students first share and then write about how ability and disability have impacted their lives. The instructor then introduces a definition of "ableism" as "the devaluation of disability" and invites students to reflect on whether this devaluation was a part of their journaling. This conversation leads to an analysis of the role of charity versus solidarity, and pity versus respect, in counseling. The last part of this session focuses on personal triggers, by (1) naming the triggers, (2) identifying their early physiological warning signs, (3) exploring their intrapersonal roots, (4) considering how they might be tied to other parts of our identities (including the gender socialization and communication patterns discussed in the first three sessions), and then (5) establishing ways students can respond to them intentionally (versus reactively) (O'Bear, 2016).

When we talked about idealized self-image [see Session 5 below], fear and insecurities, and our core self, this concept linked with my triggers. The types of things that trigger me directly bring my fears and insecurities to the foreground. Then I become defensive, since I see this as an attack on my idealized self-image. Even though this is a new discovery for me, it is one of the important ones that I have made while in the counseling program. This idealized self-image has driven many of my decisions, both good and bad.

Process: Once again, the time invested in building a "container" and honoring connections within the class is critical for establishing a supportive space in which students can self-reflect. That is why every person is required to share in the introductory activities. As with Session 1, the second set of Labs begins with a module on ability/disability because, like gender, it is a relatively unthreatening topic, and it provides the opportunity to challenge students to step outside their comfort zones as they consider how helping professionals (such as themselves) often act out of "ableist" assumptions and attitudes. In this process, the instructor invites students to review a blog post by an autistic woman, who asks to be called "autistic" rather than "a woman with autism." Students are challenged to consider a disability-rights perspective in which it is not the "disabled" who are problematic, it is the able-bodied-centric world in which we live that is problematic. This is a unique way of understanding how the world is structured around the needs of mainstream groups and a nonthreatening way for students to begin to notice the dynamics of mainstreams and margins on a topic that does not tend to evoke the same guilt as race or class. A review of the social power grid helps students remember all the ways that they are in the mainstream and begin connecting how power might manifest across settings and interactions.

The discussion about triggers centers on story-telling and extensive sharing. Students are encouraged to think about triggers in their roles as counselors, or as students studying to be counselors. The aim in this process is to have students experience triggers in the moment, as they re-evoke them, thereby working actively on strategies to recognize them and engage with them. The homework for Session 5 is to write a three-page reflection on their class background (using common definitions provided by the instructor), and how it influences their behavior, attitudes, and assumptions.

Session 5: Idealized Self-Image (Theme: Class)

Content: Students are invited to read and briefly discuss their papers on their class background in dyads (the instructor has reviewed them in advance). The longer group debrief is framed around the idea that most people who are not middle class (either because they are poor or working class, or because they are part of the professional or owning class) feel some shame around their class background. Simply naming this phenomenon often gives students permission to share their experience of class-related shame.

This sharing is followed by an activity called the Idealized Self-Image (ISI),[6] aimed at analyzing the ways in which one's fears and insecurities lead one to project a flawless "idealized self" to the world, which is easily deflated when challenged. This exercise was developed by organizational development consultant, Lorraine Marino.

I felt like I was able to be honest about my class background and to engage in conversation about it (even going to lengths to describe triggers that initially set me off to discussing my class background in public) in a way that I never have before.

I would like to work on my ISI. It was powerful to see as we acted out what we think our idealized self, the insecurities that manifest and the core self that is underneath, how much of my core self I try to hide. Most of my anxieties stem from presenting my idealized self to the world. I did not understand this concept before class. I get caught up in presenting myself one way that I lost sight of what I value at heart. It served as an anchor for me to remember what I believe in, to follow my heart and focus on building on my core self rather than what others want or expect me to be.

Process: At this point in the Labs, it does not take much for students to share personally and powerfully with one another. After students share their papers on class in dyads, the instructor asks students (i) how it *felt* to share their papers and

[6] Lorraine Marino developed the ISI awareness tool based on the Pathwork teachings of Eva Pierrakos and the 50–50 work of Moira Shaw. For the labs, the questions have been modified to relate to counseling. They are these: (1) What is your Idealized Self Image (ISI), particularly as a person studying to be a counselor? How do you insist others should see you? (2) What fears and insecurities are underneath your ISI? What does your ISI protect or cover up? (3) What is the core truth in you, the best in you, the core intentions that guide your desire to be a therapist? (4) What is the impact of your ISI on your ability to be a good counselor or therapist? Readers interested in conducting this activity should contact the first author.

hear about others' experiences, (ii) what they learned about themselves through this assignment, and (iii) how their class experiences might impact their counseling relationships. Some of the common dilemmas emerging from this discussion include: stereotypes of people on welfare; struggles to empathize with wealthy people who need therapy; shame about their own class backgrounds; how the shifting economic circumstances of young adults do not necessarily mean a change in one's "class culture;" the buffer that parents can provide and the difference it makes when one does not have that buffer; classist assumptions they make, strategies they can use to avoid classist assumptions, and the ways that class is usually intersectional with race, gender identity, and ability.

The process of having students examine their ISIs dovetails on the "triggers" activity of the prior session. Triggers are often connected to the ideal we wish to embody, and the fears or insecurities that feed such an idealized and unrealistic version of self. The goal of the ISI activity is for students to identify their "idealized selves," realize the cost of maintaining such a perfect image, and find greater freedom to act from their "core selves" (buried beneath their idealized self). When discussing the ISI, the instructor invites students to "act out" all the components of their ISI (Idealized Self-Image, Fears and Insecurities, Core Self) with a gesture and a noise[7]; students often hesitate at first, but this process helps solidify a concrete image of what is otherwise an abstract psychological concept. The session ends with sharing about how the ISI might impact students' work with clients. The assignment for the final session of the Labs asks students to reflect on their development in the Labs.

Session 6: Taking Action (Theme: Sexuality)

Content: This final session is designed to integrate the work from all prior sessions of the Labs to assist students in developing a personal understanding of intersectionality. The session begins with sharing gender identity and sexuality stories in pairs by responding to prompts such as "Describe an early memory when you understood that there were particular behavioral or attitudinal expectations of you because of your gender" or "Describe how your parents or other family members influenced your beliefs about sexual orientation" (Adams, Bell, & Griffin, 2007). Then, the instructor invites students to brainstorm how homophobia hurts everyone, using an assigned reading as a springboard (Blumenfeld, 2000). Even though the reading is not recent, it is critical for demonstrating that oppression does not only negatively impact the oppressed. This brainstorm forms the basis for a larger discussion of how each of the different types of oppression covered in the Labs (e.g., racism, sexism, transphobia, islamophobia, homophobia, ableism, classism, etc.) hurt everyone. In this process, the class identifies what it means to be an ally or an accomplice (as opposed to simply a friend, for example) and to use one's privilege to work against

---

[7] This experiential aspect of the ISI exercise was developed by Sarah Halley.

oppression. If time allows, the students are invited to practice responding to oppressive statements by taking concrete action. This final session closes with everyone sharing one takeaway and one remaining question from the Labs.

Coming from a devout Christian upbringing I had some prior knowledge about sexuality and how it differs from person to person. However, I now recognize how sexuality, particularly homosexuality, can affect clients not only on a personal level, but also on a systemic level. During my MC labs, as well as the multiculturalism course, I have had the opportunity to understand and take into account the experience of one who may identify as a homosexual. For me growing up in a black, Christian household, this has been somewhat of a taboo topic. It is interesting to finally have open dialogue about some of issues that exist within our society regarding sexuality.

Process: Students tend to be uncomfortable with the notion that homophobia hurts straight people, or that racism hurts White people. They fear undermining the experience of oppression or suggesting that oppression hurts people who are privileged as much as it hurts people who are oppressed. The instructor invites students to investigate the value of recognizing how oppression ultimately negatively impacts people from mainstream groups, thus leading students to understand how we are all operating under a larger "system" that seeks to divide us, disempower us, and sometimes teaches us to hate ourselves or each other. Through this discussion, students come to experience their interconnection and interdependence on one another, which in turn builds a felt sense of solidarity and resistance that is not simply intellectualized. Once they can see that their relationships and humanity are compromised by that "system," they develop an intrinsic interest in resisting it. During this discussion, the instructor recalls the distinctions made in earlier sessions between "charity" vs. "solidarity" and "savior" vs. "ally." We use the quote, "If you have come here to help me, you are wasting your time; but if you have come here because your liberation is bound up with mine, let us work together"[8] to prompt the students to see the ways that oppression hurts everyone. For example, if men want to fight sexism because they think women cannot do it themselves, they think women need them, or they think women are not assertive enough, they are approaching their anti-sexism from a sexist and patronizing position; but if they want to end sexism because it constricts their opportunities too—by telling them they cannot cry, by compromising their loving and emotional relationships with other men and with their children—then they have a self-interest and a position of solidarity from which to fight patriarchy and sexism and to do so in an anti-sexist way. This final Lab session is meant to leave students empowered to see others' struggles as their own and to take action. It is also designed to emphasize that the journey does not end with the Labs, but that they now have the tools to continue asking poignant questions and therefore lead their personal and professional lives in more intentional ways.

[8] This quote is often attributed to an aboriginal activist named Lila Watson.

Facilitating for Process

The Labs provide a setting in students' busy lives—where space for reflection and connection is scarce—to experience growth and transformation. The *content* of the Labs matters, in that it provides a conceptual framework leading students to recognize and describe their internal processes; for example, it introduces social identities that many students do not regularly think about, especially if they experience those identities from a position in the mainstream. However, it is the *process* used to convey such curriculum that allows for personal transformation to occur. The content facilitates the process, but it is not transformational in and of itself.

As we mentioned above, students could have an intellectualized understanding of multiculturalism without the ability to recognize its meaning and function in their own lives and therefore the lives of their clients. Self-awareness is the ground from which knowledge and skills can sprout and adapt to the terrain they find around them; it provides students with the inner compass needed to implement the knowledge and skills they have acquired in their training. Not only does self-awareness not automatically follow from knowledge and skills, but while the latter can be imparted, the former requires personal investment. Knowledge and skills can be shown and can be mimicked; self-awareness cannot be acquired by copying another's speech or behavior, and it cannot be faked. This means that self-awareness is at once essential and difficult to facilitate.

For this reason, it is important to allow for the *possibility* that students may receive an incomplete in the Labs, even when they attend all the sessions, actively participate in discussions, and do the homework. For some students, mainstream identities are too elusive; others cannot bring themselves to be honest about their triggers. In most cases, when students fail to develop adequate self-awareness, it is because they either struggle so deeply with the pain of their marginalized identities that they cannot see their own blind spots, or conversely, their privileged identities are so prominent that they cannot see the role that marginalized identities might have played in their lives or the lives of others. The former situation is particularly delicate when the instructor challenges a student who has experienced much oppression to recognize the ways in which they too have privilege and unquestioned assumptions. Yet it is imperative that students who are actively injured by the world and currently in pain find some degree of healing before they do counseling work, just as it is imperative that students who have experienced much privilege don't invalidate the experience of others for whom their marginalized identities posed more risks. Both pain and privilege can blind us to the hurt of others. As counselors, we are called to see just that. That said, it is important to note that the Labs take place early in the program and only meet six times. Judging whether a student has progressed in their self-awareness in developmentally appropriate ways is no easy feat. When adequate development appears lacking, the faculty crafts individual remediation plans (in collaboration with the program director, if needed); these may go from simply writing an addendum to the final paper to requiring additional formal or informal training.

Once all of the structural requirements are in place to elicit student participation, how does an instructor facilitate and fuel authentic engagement so that self-awareness can indeed emerge? On the one hand, there is what she does; on the other, there is who she is. The facilitator of self-awareness labs *facilitates* the group, rather than teaching or instructing. Behaviorally, she follows the energy, emotional engagement, genuineness, puzzlement, and confusion in the students' verbal and nonverbal behaviors, often by trusting her own felt sense of engagement as a thermometer (e.g., are students asking questions, itching to speak, watching the speaker or each other intently?) Class sessions are structured around the specific examples from students' lives that they write about in their papers; this fosters mutual vulnerability and story-telling. When students bring their different truths and experiences into the discussion, they create a space that differs markedly from their typical classrooms in which it is primarily their theories and ideas that are valued. Students are invited to enter and reflect upon disagreements (e.g., to reflect on the meaning of the conflict, their internal reactions to the conflict)—and to recognize conflict as a potential source of growth. Students are also invited to sit with silences, which provide critical space for students to process new feelings or new perspectives. Needless to say, fostering authentic connections among the students and with the instructor is a must. This is why the structure of the Labs is designed for students to engage deeply with themselves and one another, and why depth of discussion is always preferred over breadth of material covered.

What then enables the instructor to perform effectively the above behaviors? As a facilitator, she brings herself fully to the Labs, including her own self-awareness and the requisite ego-strength to be *in process* herself. The instructor's ability to share her own mainstream identities, life experiences, and growth process models genuine vulnerability, which in turn fosters trust and greater authenticity from the students. In other words, the instructor is to students' self-awareness, what a counselor is to the therapeutic relationship.

This calls for ongoing reflection, growth, and consultation on the part of the instructor. For example, it is important for the instructor not to over-share as well as to monitor the impact of her sharing, as the only way for students to grow their self-awareness is to do the work *themselves*. Over-sharing can overshadow that process and turn the instructor into a "specimen" for students to analyze or imitate. Further, some of what the instructor shares is a relatively new awareness, and therefore affectively charged, while much of what she shares is well-integrated into her identity, thus less triggering in the moment. Over-sharing what is not yet integrated into her identity can weaken the "container" needed for students to learn and grow, as the instructor's groundedness is part of what creates that container.

In conclusion, just like in counseling, it is what we bring to our students and to MC work as instructors that is transformational. When it comes to assisting students to develop self-awareness, it is not as much *what* we teach, but how much of our own experiential wisdom and authenticity we are able bring to our teaching. If we succeed, students leave the Labs with the (often new) experience of being part of an honest, diverse, conscious community. They come away from the Labs not only *seeing* that such a community is possible, but also knowing what it *feels* like to be a part of one. When such awareness is coupled with knowledge and skills, they are indeed transformed into agents of change for their clients and their communities.

References

Bartoli, E., Bentley-Edwards, K. L., García, A. M., Michael, A., & Ervin, A. (2015). What do white counselors need to know about race? White racial socialization in counseling and psychotherapy training programs. *Women & Therapy, 38*, 246–262.

Bartoli, E., Morrow, M., Dozier, C. G., Mamolou, A., & Gillem, A. R. (2014). Creating effective counselors: Integrated multicultural and evidence-based curricula in counselor education programs. *Journal of the Pennsylvania Counseling Association, 13*(1), 27–38.

Blumenfeld, W. J. (2000). How homophobia hurts everyone. In M. Adams, W. J. Blumenfeld, R. Castaneda, H. W. Hackman, M. L. Peters, & X. Zuniga (Eds.), *Readings for diversity and social justice* (pp. 267–275). London: Routledge.

David-Russell, E. (2003). Integrating multicultural issues into graduate clinical psychology training. In P. Bronstein & K. Quina (Eds.), *Teaching gender and multicultural awareness: Resources for the psychology classroom* (pp. 339–346). Washington, DC: American Psychological Association.

O'Bear, K. (2016). *Turn the tide*. Washington, DC: Difference Press.

Rogers, M. R., & O'Bryon, E. C. (2014). Multicultural training models and curriculum. In F. T. L. Leong (Ed.), *APA handbook of multicultural psychology, Applications and training* (Vol. 2, pp. 659–679). Washington, DC: American Psychological Association.

Project Implicit. (n.d.). *Implicit Attitudes Test (IAT)*.. https://implicit.harvard.edu/implicit/takeatest.html

Ross, H. J. (2014). *Everyday bias: Identifying and navigating unconscious judgments in our daily lives*. Lanham: Rowman & Littlefield.

Singleton, G. E., & Linton, C. W. (2015). *Courageous conversations about race: A field guide for achieving equity in schools*. Thousand Oakes: Corwin Press.

Sue, D. W., & Sue, D. (2013). *Counseling the culturally diverse: Theory and practice* (6th ed.). New York, NY: Wiley.

Williams, E. N., Hayes, J. A., & Fauth, J. (2008). Therapist self-awareness: Interdisciplinary connection and future directions. In D. S. Brown & R. W. Lent (Eds.), *Handbook of counseling psychology* (4th ed., pp. 303–319). Hoboken, NJ: Wiley.

Developing Cultural Awareness and Sensitivity through Simulation

Toula Kourgiantakis and Marion Bogo

Students in counseling-related programs work with culturally diverse individuals, families, and communities and educational programs need to help students develop a comprehensive understanding of the multifaceted ways culture impacts mental health and well-being, as well as the helping relationship (Falender & Shafranske, 2007; Hardy, 2016). Professions such as social work (CSWE, 2015), counseling (ACA, 2014), marriage, and family therapy (AAMFT, 2004), as well as psychology (APA, 2002) have developed standards for cultural competence that are used as guidelines for educational programs. These standards are often embedded in a larger set of competencies that are discipline-specific (Gehart, 2011). While specific disciplines use different terms, most recognize that culture is complex, "pervasive and influential" and it has been defined as a "broad-based multidimensional concept that is comprised of, but not limited to, race, class, religion, sexual orientation, gender, family of origin, ethnicity, age, regionality" (Hardy, 2016, p. 4).

Although professional organizations are explicitly committed to practitioners developing cultural competence, in recent years educators and researchers have raised concerns about the adequacy of teaching and professional training related to diversity and culture across several professions (Falender & Shafranske, 2007; Hardy & Bobes, 2016; Inman, Meza, Brown, & Hargrove, 2004). Educational programs must enhance the teaching of both cultural awareness and cultural sensitivity. Cultural awareness indicates *what* we know about culture, while cultural sensitivity refers to *how* we address or respond to cultural dimensions (Hardy, 2016).

This need to enhance the teaching of cultural awareness and sensitivity has informed our curriculum development and teaching at the Factor-Inwentash Faculty of Social Work at the University of Toronto. We have been committed to enhancing

T. Kourgiantakis (✉) • M. Bogo
Factor-Inwentash Faculty of Social Work, University of Toronto,
Toronto, M5S 1V4 ON, Canada
e-mail: toula.kourgiantakis@utoronto.ca; marion.bogo@utoronto.ca

R. Allan, S.S. Poulsen (eds.), *Creating Cultural Safety in Couple and Family Therapy*, AFTA SpringerBriefs in Family Therapy,
DOI 10.1007/978-3-319-64617-6_8

clinical competency development in the classroom and linking this with student learning in practice settings. We have found that students have difficulty conceptualizing and responding to cultural components of clinical interventions and our simulation program has been an innovative teaching method to address these learning needs. We (T.K. and M.B.) are both faculty members and simulation-based learning is the signature pedagogy of our graduate program. Toula is a social worker and family therapist and second-generation Greek-Canadian. I have spent most of my career working in clinical settings with diverse populations in both official languages of Canada. Prior to working in an academic setting, I worked with diverse families and supervised diverse students in French and English in schools, child welfare and mental health agencies, and in each context, saw how important it was to understand one's own cultural selves in order to develop greater cultural sensitivity with others. This has been an important part of my teaching and supervision, but was not without challenges in terms of how to enhance this learning experience for students. This has shaped my work as Simulation Coordinator at the faculty.

Marion is a professor of social work and couple therapist and third-generation Canadian-Jewish woman. I have worked in Montreal and Toronto in Canada, as well as Ohio, in community, mental health, and private settings. As the population of Canada became more diverse, I became more aware of the lack of systematic training for cultural responsiveness in social work practice. Through my clinical and educational research, it became clear that teaching with simulation provided a focused approach to applying theory to practice including developing cultural sensitivity.

In this chapter, we will discuss how simulation-based learning can help address some of the challenges of teaching and assessing cultural awareness and sensitivity in counseling programs. We will review some of the criticisms that have been raised about competency-based education and how this has influenced our simulation program. We will subsequently discuss how some of these concerns can be addressed through the use of simulation in the teaching and assessment of clinical competencies (specifically cultural awareness and sensitivity) in the counseling-related professions. The chapter will delineate *what* students learn through simulation and *how* students learn through this method. It will also describe how to develop and implement simulation-based learning opportunities in professional training programs. We will provide examples from our experiences of teaching and assessing graduate students using simulation with the collaboration of supervisors from community practice settings.

Simulation as an Enhancement in Teaching and Learning

Simulation is an experiential teaching method that replicates real clinician-client sessions and appears authentic for students (Gaba, 2007). Students interact with trained actors in carefully designed scenarios typical of those encountered in counseling-related professions. Guided by a clinical instructor or supervisor, students can build practice knowledge and skills and experience systematic reflection on their internal cognitive and affective states that influence their practice. Simulation is a meaningful form of experiential learning where we give students specific feedback that they purposefully reflect upon and this contributes to changes in many areas including judgment, emotions, and skills.

At the Factor-Inwentash Faculty of Social Work, we were interested in developing alternate ways of assessing students' competence in social work practice; therefore, we studied and adapted the Objective Structured Clinical Examination (OSCE) widely used in health professions. During an OSCE, students interview simulated clients, while their practice is observed and rated by an instructor. To prepare students for the OSCE, we began increasingly teaching with simulation and noted its powerful impact on student learning as it provides practice for students, an opportunity for clinical instructors to give immediate feedback on specific skills, and students also learn to link abstract concepts to practice behaviors. In addition, observing students' challenges in responding to culture and diversity during simulations provided us with information about gaps in our own teaching (Bogo, Rawlings, Katz, & Logie, 2014).

There are several other advantages of simulation-based learning opportunities including increasing students' confidence for real practice situations. Well-developed simulations in a safe space also encourage students to take risks and step outside of their comfort zones, with no adverse effects on actual clients. Hardy and Bobes (2016) describe experiential learning as the "hallmark of supervision and training designed to promote cultural sensitivity" (p. viii) as this facilitates greater awareness of cultural identities and purposeful use of self with clients.

Concerns and Challenges with a Cultural Competency Framework

Our simulation program is guided by a competency-based framework which is conducive for teaching and learning cultural awareness and sensitivity (Falender & Shafranske, 2007). This model focuses on student learning and performance outcomes, as well as program outcomes. In many disciplines, there has been an implicit assumption that competencies are attained simply by virtue of program completion, but there has been a recent shift with a call for explicit demonstration of competence (Miller, Todahl, & Platt, 2010). Educators and researchers have found that there are challenges integrating cultural competencies in programs and curricula (Inman et al., 2004) as there may not be opportunities to demonstrate these competencies in the classroom. There are also concerns that this is a reductionist approach that simplifies the concept "culture" and focuses on proclivities of specific groups (Bogo et al., 2006; Hardy, 2016). In addition to the fact that cultural competence is an abstract concept, not having a unified definition of cultural competence makes it more challenging for educators to integrate this in educational and clinical programs. Researchers and clinicians have argued that it is imperative to include intersectionality in any conceptualization of cultural competence and they underline that students need to explore their own social identities in order to increase self-awareness of assumptions, biases, and values. Academic settings tend to overemphasize cultural content and have insufficient emphasis on critical self-reflection and cultural sensitivity (Laszloffy & Habekost, 2010).

Conceptual Framework: Development of Holistic Competence in Students

Our professional competence model has been a product of several studies led by the second author (MB) along with colleagues and researchers from other institutions. These studies (involving both students and supervisors) have shown that some professional competence models are too narrow with a focus on discrete components of knowledge, skills, values, and attitudes and they overlook crucial dimensions of clinical competence such as tacit knowledge, biases, assumptions, values, and emotional reactions (Bogo et al., 2011). These dimensions are requisites of cultural sensitivity (Hardy, 2016; Laszloffy & Habekost, 2010). Previous research findings and ongoing observation of our students in simulated learning activities have shown that students have difficulty not only in the demonstration of micro skills (also known as procedural competencies), but also in linking practice with relevant theories, regulating affect in sessions, using purposeful and intentional interventions, and also showing a strong level of self-awareness (Bogo et al., 2013). Supervisors also describe that they evaluate students not only on specific assessment and counseling skills, but also on students' approach to learning, as well as their ability to conceptualize their practice and the level of professionalism demonstrated by the student at the internship setting (Bogo et al., 2006). These research findings led to the development of the holistic competence model (see Fig. 1), which we use as a conceptual framework in the teaching and assessment of clinical skills at the faculty (Bogo et al., 2014).

The holistic model includes both procedural *and* meta-competencies; procedural competencies comprise micro-clinical skills such as the ability to form a collaborative helping relationship, conduct an assessment, and implement interventions, while meta-competencies refer to the ability to be introspective and this relies on self-regulation, self-reflection, and self-awareness (Bogo et al., 2014). The holistic model has four interrelated specific dimensions shaped by contextual factors such as each profession's values and ethics, as well as community characteristics and the organizational mandate in which clinical practice occurs. In one quadrant, the model illustrates *knowledge* that includes theoretical and empirical knowledge, as well as tacit knowledge derived from personal and professional experiences. Another quadrant features *skills* that are used to execute complex practice behaviors. *Judgment* is in a third quadrant and refers to the way students use knowledge to conceptualize

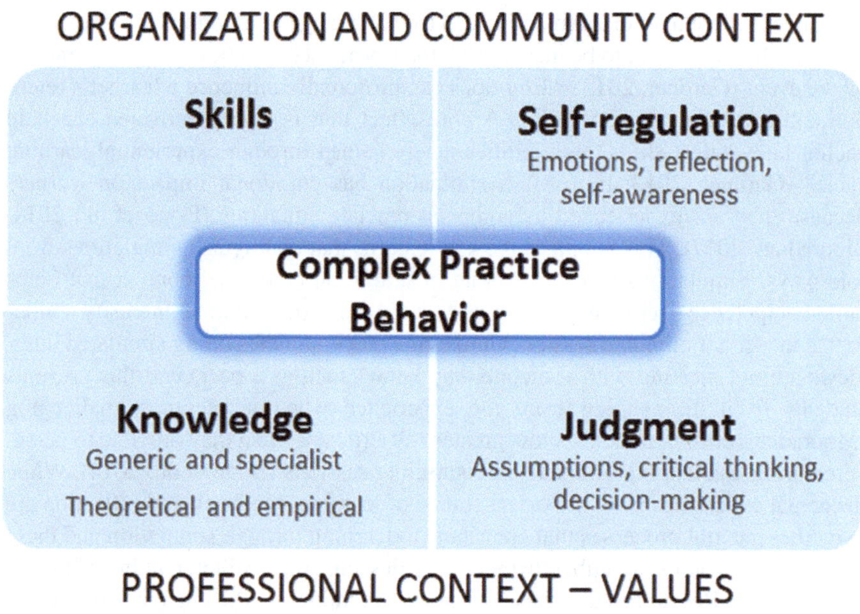

Fig. 1 Reprinted with permission of the Council on Social Work Education from Bogo et al. (2014). *Using simulation in assessment and teaching: OSCE adapted for social work.* Alexandria, VI: Council on Social Work Education

their practice and engage in critical thinking and self-reflection about their assumptions and biases. The final quadrant is *self-regulation* and it comprises awareness of emotional states and emotional regulation. Together, judgment and self-regulation have a critical influence on decision-making and intervention. Using this holistic competence model as a framework guides us in identifying competencies that draw from all four dimensions for our simulation-based learning activities.

The Learning Process in Simulation

Simulation is conducive for learning in a professional program and it is congruent with adult learning principles (Knowles, 1968) and Kolb's (1984) experiential learning theory. Students arrive in a clinical learning context with a set of assumptions, personal experiences, personal characteristics, knowledge, emotions, and cognitions that shape their actions. Experiential learning allows students to transform previous experiences and create new learning in all of the spheres of the holistic competence model (knowledge, skills, self-awareness, self-regulation, judgment). A well-designed simulation provides an opportunity to combine an active experience with reflection on the practice through focused debriefing (Gardner, 2013).

Active involvement in a simulation can trigger a range of emotions for learners. In order for the experience to be meaningful, the learner needs to be emotionally moved by the event (Gardner, 2013). "Emotions can profoundly influence a learner's retention and activation of knowledge. A core affect that is highly activated can help anchor knowledge, skills, and abilities newly gained through experiential-learning cycle" (Gardner, 2013, p. 168). A simulation has emotional impact on learners because they are experienced as authentic practice situations (Bogo et al., 2014; Mooradian, 2007). This is one of the key features that distinguish simulations from role plays. Simulations can be accurate in setting an emotional context that helps build competence. Actors are able to use a wide range of emotional intensity similar to that in a client-clinician session. Unlike role plays, students doing simulated interviews are not meeting with someone they know (such as a peer) and this prevents students from disengaging from the experience when it becomes challenging (Mooradian, 2007). Students show greater self-efficacy when they are able to persevere during challenging moments in counseling sessions (Bogo et al., 2014). While the actual experience is an important source of learning, feedback and reflection are two other integral processes that contribute to learning through simulation and these are core components of deliberate practice (Ericsson, 2008; Miller, Hubble, Chow, & Seidel, 2013). Recent research has shown that practitioners who engage in deliberate practice have superior clinical performance (Miller et al., 2013).

Reflection is described as the "cornerstone" of experiential learning (Fanning & Gaba, 2007; Kolb, 1984). Reflection is a critical analysis of one's own practice, as well as the practice of others in order to have a deeper understanding of the experience. The role of reflection in simulation-based learning draws on the work of Dewey (1933) in educational theory, Kolb (1984) in experiential learning, and Schön (1987) who related reflective work to professional practice. Professional practice situations are often complex, multifaceted, and may involve ethical dilemmas. Schön (1987) explained that learners use "knowing-in-action" or tacit/implicit knowledge that underpins and accompanies action and also guides work in complex situations. We could also refer to this as professional judgment. When students face situations that are unfamiliar (this can include uncomfortable feelings and thoughts for the learner), they engage in a process called "reflection-in-action" that shapes a situation and how the learner responds to it (Schön 1987, p. 26). Reflection-in-action occurs because the learner's knowing-in-action is inadequate to respond to the practice. During reflection-in-action, learners use critical thinking and question assumptions (Bogo et al., 2014). The next dimension of professional practice is referred to as "reflection-on action" where learners reflect back on their practice, critically appraise it, and may consider other responses or make changes for future interactions (Schön, 1987). The role of a supervisor or clinical instructor is paramount in facilitating this reflective process (Fanning & Gaba, 2007). Supervisors elicit information about the experience from students and they also provide feedback to facilitate reflection by students on areas that require greater development. Supervisors can use the holistic competence model to guide this process as this ensures both procedural and meta-competencies are included in the reflection and feedback phases of the simulation. Clinical instructors can also integrate written reflections as part of all simulation learning activities with questions that elicit information about ways in which culture impacts different dimensions of holistic competence (knowledge, skills, self-awareness, affect regulation, and judgment). Our simulation activities often include both oral and written reflection exercises and most reflection questions explore students' ability to self-reflect, self-assess, and show self-awareness. Students can find it challenging to reflect on cultural factors influencing the interview (their own cultural selves, as well as that of the client), but this is an invaluable part of the learning experience. We have found that some students require additional support to better understand and describe their own emotions, values, assumptions, and biases. When supervisors or clinical instructors give students focused feedback, this can facilitate student reflection and enhance learning.

Feedback is the second integral part of student learning in simulation activities. A systematic review on medical simulation literature identified feedback as the most important part of simulation-based learning (Issenberg, McGaghie, Petrusa, Gordon, & Scalese, 2005). Feedback provides students with a better understanding of the factors contributing to a client's situation, as well as the factors influencing students' affective, cognitive, and behavioral responses to the client (Fanning & Gaba, 2007). Through increased self-awareness, students are able to use the self in an intentional, purposeful manner.

Supervisors, educators, and researchers have emphasized the invaluable role of feedback in student learning, yet there is a paucity of research on feedback (Gardner, 2013), particularly in specific areas such as corrective feedback (Bogo et al., 2006) and cross-cultural issues (Burkard, Knox, Clarke, Phelps, & Inman, 2014). Moreover, the lack of immediate, specific, and constructive feedback has been identified as the most significant barrier in deliberate practice (Bogo, Regehr, Power, & Regehr, 2007; Miller et al., 2013). Many students in professional programs receive a part of their training in a practice setting where they are supervised and evaluated by a professional in the field and some supervisors show reticence in providing corrective feedback (Bogo et al., 2007; Burkard et al., 2014). Providing corrective feedback and being in a gatekeeping role may sometimes collide with a supervisor's professional values that are linked with diversity, strengths, and empowerment (Bogo et al., 2007).

There are many factors that facilitate giving corrective feedback such as the relationship between supervisor-student and the student's openness in receiving and applying feedback (Bogo et al., 2007). Burkard et al. (2014) found that cultural differences between supervisor-student influence the feedback process and so does the type of cultural content being discussed. There are several other characteristics that contribute to effective feedback such as giving specific, clear, timely, and ongoing feedback to students, incorporating self-reflection in the feedback process, creating a safe environment (Gardner, 2013), and having a supervisor or clinical instructor who includes all of these characteristics in his/her feedback while using person-centered skills such as empathy, congruence, and acceptance (Fanning & Gaba, 2007).

Feedback and reflection exercises are integrated in all of our simulations, but they can have different formats depending on factors such as group size, time constraints, whether the activity is graded, as well as the learning/teaching styles of students and instructors. Clinical instructors usually provide feedback to students immediately after their simulated interviews and we sometimes stop a simulated interview at mid-point in order to provide feedback and allow the student to resume the interview and implement the feedback. Peers can also give feedback during simulation learning activities, but a supervisor or clinical instructor should guide this feedback, so it is specific, calibrated (positive and corrective feedback), respectful, and related to targeted competencies. The learning experience of "peer observers" in a simulation can be enhanced when the clinical instructor purposefully engages the observers. Students who are not in the clinician role during a simulation can informally assess their peers' simulated interviews and rate the extent to which they observed competencies (using Likert-type and open-ended questions). Our students show greater engagement in an activity when they are asked to identify specific competencies in their peers and they learn to provide feedback using strengths-based and culturally sensitive approaches. Cultural attunement and sensitivity are competencies in all of our simulations and cultural components are part of all group discussions and reflection exercises.

Assessment of Holistic Competence in Simulation-Based Learning

Educators using competency-based frameworks in professional programs are seeking reliable and valid methods to assess educational outcomes. There are two forms of assessment in learner-centered education. The first is formative assessment which provides students with feedback to improve learning and performance using learner-centered methods and can be conceived as assessment *for* learning. At the University of Toronto, we use video recorded and live simulated interviews as two methods of formative assessment. Many courses have in-class simulation exercises where students practice interviewing a simulated client. In one of our foundation year courses, students are also required to prepare a video-recorded simulated interview with a peer along with a written reflective analysis of the interview. They are not graded for these activities, but they receive ample oral and written feedback on the competencies demonstrated in the simulated interviews and in their written reflections.

The second form of assessment is summative and this is often conducted at the end of a course. A summative assessment emphasizes outcome-based methods and can be conceived as assessment *of* learning (Bogo et al., 2014; Gehart, 2011). The most authentic evaluation of practice ability is observation and assessment of students while they are involved in actual practice. One example of a summative assessment is the Objective Structured Clinical Examination (OSCE) and we use this to assess holistic competence (including cultural sensitivity) (Bogo et al., 2011).

The OSCE started in medicine to assess the clinical skills and competence of medical students (Harden, Stevenson, Downie, & Wilson, 1975), but it is now used by many other health care programs. OSCEs involve the use of standardized clients trained to simulate and enact a clinical situation in a standardized manner. A clinical instructor writes vignettes that resemble authentic client situations seen in clinical practice. The OSCE is a valuable evaluation method, as it does not have the same variability when evaluating practice with actual clients, thus providing a standardized and equitable approach to evaluating students' competence.

There has been a dearth of research on the use of OSCEs outside of health care. At the University of Toronto, we have conducted several studies on adapting and using OSCEs to assess complex competencies in graduate social work students (Bogo et al., 2011). Designing an OSCE is a four-step iterative process and there are similar steps involved when teaching competencies using simulation. The first step is identifying competencies and practice behaviors with observable indicators. This may be the most challenging step, but it must not be omitted as it is the foundation of the simulated learning process. Clinical instructors can create a competency matrix that outlines what students need to demonstrate, what they will need to possess in order to demonstrate these competencies (knowledge, skills, values, cognitive, and affective processes), and how they will demonstrate these competencies (indicators). The second step in developing an OSCE is mapping the competencies and related practice behaviors to a potential case scenario. The case scenario should include specific issues and client characteristics because these will provide opportunities for students to demonstrate the practice behavior related to that competency. The third step involves writing a vignette that resembles authentic practice. The vignette should give background information about the client, the client's systems, and should also describe cultural/structural factors affecting the client. Information is given about the client's emotional state, verbatim items to be used by the standardized clients, and goals for the student. The clinical instructor uses this case description to prepare the simulation and train the actor. Students receive a brief client summary that includes information about the service setting, client referral, role of the clinician, focus of the interview, identifying client information, and a synopsis about the presenting concern. The final step in designing an OSCE is developing a rating scale to assess student competencies (Bogo et al., 2014).

An actual OSCE has a structured procedure where students read a brief written synopsis of the case scenario and then proceed to conduct an interview with the standardized client described in the scenario. A clinical instructor observes the interview and rates the student on a number of competencies (Bogo et al., 2014). At the end of the interview, the student is given some feedback on his/her interview and then the student responds to a set of written reflection questions. The written reflection questions ask students to describe the theories, concepts, or models that influenced their practice in the interview. Students are also asked to discuss professional and personal experiences that shaped their understanding of the client and client's situation. Another question focuses on students' emotions during the interview and how emotions were regulated. Students also need to write about challenging moments during the session and how they coped with the challenges. The reflection questionnaire also asks students to discuss the way culture impacted the interview and we emphasize that they need to reflect on their own cultural selves, as well as the clients' cultural selves. The clinical instructor uses another rating scale to evaluate students' reflections. Our research examining OSCEs for the last 7 years has shown that using the holistic competence framework (described in a previous section) makes this a more rigorous assessment method. It permits clinical instructors to assess many dimensions of procedural competence such as alliance building, conducting an assessment, cultural awareness and sensitivity, and setting collaborative intervention goals. Cultural awareness and sensitivity is both a procedural and meta-competency. As a procedural competency, the clinical instructor assesses *what* the student does and *how* this is done by the student. The post-OSCE reflection exercise permits clinical instructors to assess students' meta-competencies such as conceptualization of practice, critical thinking, judgments and decision-making processes, use of self, as well as emotion regulation. When rating cultural awareness and sensitivity as a meta-competency, some of the areas clinical instructors are assessing include, but are not limited to, students' assumptions, self-awareness, reflexivity, intentionality, and purposeful use of self (Bogo et al., 2014).

Simulation as a Signature Pedagogy

Recent research studies conducted at our faculty have found that simulation facilitates the development of holistic competence and this has contributed to the growth of our simulation program over the last 10 years (Bogo et al., 2011, 2014). In addition to using simulation to teach foundation year students about assessment and interviewing skills, we also use simulation to teach advanced clinical competencies in specialized areas such as mental health, primary health care, substance use, suicide risk assessment, mindfulness, mediation, child protection, group work, gerontology, and family therapy. In a foundation year practice course, we teach students generic clinical competencies using simulation, and at the end of the course, competency attainment is assessed using an OSCE. Procedural and meta-competencies are taught throughout the course using various methods such as simulated interviews and assessments with standardized clients. We have also developed teaching resources (such as videos) that present supervisors/clinicians from our affiliated agencies as they demonstrate clinical skills and conduct assessments with standardized clients. We recently piloted a simulation with the collaboration of a mental health agency on how to conduct a mental health assessment. We are also in the early stages of developing a simulation that will focus on macro matters such as advocacy and policy development.

As mentioned previously, we have a relatively new voluntary simulation activity referred to as "Practice Fridays." Practice Fridays offer students an opportunity to participate in simulated interviews and assessments focusing on different areas and we invite a supervisor from a community agency to each Practice Friday. This permits us to bridge classroom and clinical practice in our teaching and assessment of procedural and meta-competencies. Supervisors are able to share their clinical expertise and give feedback to students on clinical skill development. We are also able to provide supervisors with a framework that they can use to teach and assess competencies, as well as a model for giving students more focused feedback. In our Practice Friday, students reported that simulation activities enhanced all four dimensions of holistic competence (skills, knowledge, self-regulation, and judgment). Students attributed their learning to a few processes including the opportunity to practice, having safety in the group, engaging in critical self-reflection, and receiving focused and immediate feedback by the clinical instructor, supervisor, and fellow peers. Cultural awareness and sensitivity are core competencies in all of our simulations and we can see that this is not a linear learning process. We are continuing to gather feedback from our students, fellow faculty members, external supervisors, as well as our Diversity and Equity Advisor to evaluate how we can help students develop these competencies both in the classroom and in practice.

In summary, our research and practice demonstrate that a number of important elements are needed for a simulation to be a substantive teaching and assessment method in counseling-related professions. These indispensable elements discussed in the aforementioned sections of the chapter include the following: (1) a conceptual framework such as the model of holistic competence, (2) clearly identified competencies, (3) a comprehensive vignette that maps the competencies, (4) well-trained actor(s), (5) a clinical instructor to organize and facilitate the simulation activity, (6) an assessment rating scale (if applicable), (7) immediate, specific, and calibrated feedback for students, (8) oral and written reflection exercises, (9) teaching methods to intentionally engage students when they are in observer roles, and (10) collaboration with supervisors in practice settings.

Conclusion

Although many professional associations and accrediting bodies have developed cultural competencies or standards, there is still a gap that exists between what students need and what they receive in educational and training programs. This often results in students not being adequately prepared for clinical practice when they commence internships. Simulation is an experiential teaching and assessment method that permits educators to address and overcome many of the concerns about cultural competency frameworks. Simulation-based learning is not a single course approach to teaching cultural awareness and sensitivity. This teaching method can be integrated in most courses and across an entire program, along with cultural competencies that challenge students to examine the omnipresence of culture and the manner in which culture influences power, privilege, subjugation and oppression, and all human experiences. A holistic competence model provides a foundational framework for simulation-based learning as it integrates procedural and meta-competencies, as well as the influence of contextual factors. A holistic conceptual framework combined with an experiential learning method, such as simulation, facilitates the development of cultural awareness and sensitivity in education and training. Through simulation-based learning, students have an opportunity to learn in an iterative cycle where they engage in deliberate practice, receive constructive feedback, and self-reflect on biases, assumptions, values, and other key factors that shape the helping relationship.

References

American Association for Marriage and Family Therapy. (2004). *Marriage and family therapy core competencies*. Alexandria, VA: Author. Retrieved from https://www.aamft.org/imis15/Documents/MFT_Core_Competencie.pdf

American Counseling Association. (2014). *ACA code of ethics*. Alexandria, VA: Author. Retrieved from http://www.counseling.org/docs/ethics/2014-aca-code-of-ethics.pdf?sfvrsn=4

American Psychological Association. (2002). *Guidelines on multicultural education, training, research, practice, and organizational change for psychologists*. Washington, DC: Author. Retrieved from http://www.apa.org/pi/oema/resources/policy/multicultural-guideline.pdf

Bogo, M., Katz, E., Regehr, C., Logie, C., Mylopoulos, M., & Tufford, L. (2013). Toward understanding meta-competence: An analysis of students' reflection on their simulated interviews. *Social Work Education, 32*(2), 259–273. doi:10.1080/02615479.2012.738662

Bogo, M., Rawlings, M., Katz, E., & Logie, C. (2014). *Using simulation in assessment and teaching. OSCE adapted for social work*. Alexandria, VA: CSWE Press.

Bogo, M., Regehr, C., Logie, C., Katz, E., Mylopoulos, M., & Regehr, G. (2011). Adapting objective structured clinical examinations to assess social work students' performance and reflections. *Journal of Social Work Education, 47*(1), 5–18. doi:10.5175/JSWE.2011.200900036

Bogo, M., Regehr, C., Power, R., & Regehr, G. (2007). When values collide: Providing feedback and evaluating competence in social work. *The Clinical Supervisor, 26*(1/2), 99–117. doi:10.1300/J001v26n01_08

Bogo, M., Regehr, C., Woodford, M., Hughes, J., Power, R., & Regehr, G. (2006). Beyond competencies: Field instructors' descriptions of student performance. *Journal of Social Work Education, 42*(3), 579–594. doi:10.5175/JSWE.2006.200404145

Burkard, A. W., Knox, S., Clarke, R. D., Phelps, D. L., & Inman, A. G. (2014). Supervisors' experiences of providing difficult feedback in cross-ethnic/racial supervision. *The Counseling Psychologist, 42*(3), 314–344. doi:10.1177/0011000012461157

Council of Social Work Education. (2015). *Educational policy and accreditation standards. (EPAS)*. Alexandria, VA: Author. Retrieved from http://www.cswe.org/file.aspx?id=81660

Dewey, J. (1933). *How we think*. Buffalo, NY: Heath.

Ericsson, K. A. (2008). Deliberate practice and acquisition of expert performance: A general overview. *Academic Emergency Medicine, 15*(11), 988–994. doi:10.1111/j.1553-2712.2008.00227.x

Falender, C. A., & Shafranske, E. P. (2007). Competence in competency-based supervision practice: Construct and application. *Professional Psychology: Research and Practice, 38*(3), 232–240. doi:10.1037/0735-7028.38.3.232

Fanning, R. M., & Gaba, D. M. (2007). The role of debriefing in simulation-based learning. *Simulation in Healthcare, 2*(2), 115–125. doi:10.1097/SIH.0b013e3180315539

Gaba, D. M. (2007). The future vision of simulation in healthcare. *Simulation in Healthcare, 2*(2), 126–135. doi:10.1097/01.SIH.0000258411.38212.32

Gardner, R. (2013). Introduction to debriefing. *Seminars in Perinatology, 37*(3), 166–174. doi:10.1053/j.semperi.2013.02.008

Gehart, D. (2011). The core competencies and MFT education: Practical aspects of transitioning to a learning-centered, outcome-based pedagogy. *Journal of Marital and Family Therapy, 37*(3), 344–354. doi:10.1111/j.1752-0606.2010.00205.x

Harden, R., Stevenson, M., Downie, W., & Wilson, W. (1975). Assessment of clinical competence using objective structured examination. *Medical Education, 13*, 41–54. doi:10.1136/bmj.1.5955.447

Hardy, K. (2016). Toward the development of a multicultural relational perspective in training and supervision. In K. V. Hardy & T. Bobes (Eds.), *Culturally sensitive supervision and training: Diverse perspectives and practical applications* (pp. 3–10). New York, NY: Routledge.

Hardy, K. V., & Bobes, T. (Eds.). (2016). *Culturally sensitive supervision and training: Diverse perspectives and practical applications*. New York, NY: Routledge.

Inman, A. G., Meza, M. M., Brown, A. L., & Hargrove, B. K. (2004). Student faculty perceptions of multicultural training in accredited marriage and family therapy programs in relation to students' self-reported competence. *Journal of Marital and Family Therapy, 30*(3), 373–388. doi:10.1111/j.1752-0606.2004.tb01247.x

Issenberg, S. B., McGaghie, W. C., Petrusa, E. R., Gordon, D. L., & Scalese, R. J. (2005). Features and uses of high-fidelity medical simulations that lead to effective learning: A BEME systematic review. *Medical Teacher, 27*(1), 10–28. doi:10.1080/01421590500046924

Knowles, M. S. (1968). Andragogy, not pedagogy. Adult Leadership, 16(10), 350-352., 386.

Kolb, D. A. (1984). *Experiential learning: Experience as a source of learning and development*. Englewood Cliffs, NJ: Prentice Hall.

Laszloffy, T., & Habekost, J. (2010). Using experiential tasks to enhance cultural sensitivity among MFT trainees. *Journal of Marital and Family Therapy, 36*(3), 333–346. doi:10.1111/j.1752-0606.2010.00213.x

Miller, J. K., Todahl, J. L., & Platt, J. J. (2010). The core competency movement in marriage and family therapy: Key considerations from other disciplines. *Journal of Marital and Family Therapy, 36*(1), 59–70. doi:10.1111/j.1752-0606.2009.00183.x

Miller, S. D., Hubble, M. A., Chow, D. L., & Seidel, J. A. (2013). The outcome of psychotherapy: Yesterday, today, and tomorrow. *Psychotherapy, 50*(1), 88–97. doi:10.1037/a0031097

Mooradian, J. K. (2007). Simulated family therapy interviews in clinical social work education. *Journal of Teaching in Social Work, 27*(1-2), 89–104. doi:10.1037/a0031097

Schön, D. (1987). *Educating the reflective practitioner*. San Francisco, CA: Jossey-Bass.

FSC
www.fsc.org
MIX
Papier | Fördert
gute Waldnutzung
FSC® C083411

Kolibri 360 GmbH
Ferdinand-Jühlke-Straße 7
99095 Erfurt, Deutschland
produktsicherheit@kolibri360.de